THE GERMAN SHEPHERD DOG

Diane Morgan

The German Shepherd Dog

Project Team
Editor: Stephanie Fornino
Copy Editor: Carl Schutt
Design: Tilly Grassa
Series Design: Mada Design
Series Originator: Dominique De Vito

T.F.H. Publications
President/CEO: Glen S. Axelrod
Executive Vice President: Mark E. Johnson
Publisher: Christopher T. Reggio
Production Manager: Kathy Bontz

T.F.H. Publications, Inc.
One TFH Plaza
Third and Union Avenues
Neptune City, NJ 07753

ISBN 978-0-7938-3635-2

Printed and bound in China
08 09 10 11 12   7 9 8 6

Library of Congress Cataloging-in-Publication Data
Morgan, Diane, 1947-
The German shepherd dog / Diane Morgan.
p. cm.
Includes index.
ISBN 0-7938-3635-2 (alk. paper)
1. German shepherd dog. I. Title.
SF429.G37M67 2005
636.737'6—dc22
2005007598

This book has been published with the intent to provide accurate and authoritative information in regard to the subject matter within. While every reasonable precaution has been taken in preparation of this book, the author and publisher expressly disclaim responsibility for any errors, omissions, or adverse effects arising from the use or application of the information contained herein. The techniques and suggestions are used at the reader's discretion and are not to be considered a substitute for veterinary care. If you suspect a medical problem consult your veterinarian.

The Leader In Responsible Animal Care For Over 50 Years!®
www.tfh.com

TABLE OF CONTENTS

Chapter 1
HISTORY OF THE GERMAN SHEPHERD DOG 5
Early Development of the Breed • The German Shepherd Dog in the UK •
The German Shepherd Dog Comes to America

Chapter 2
CHARACTERISTICS OF THE GERMAN SHEPHERD DOG 19
German-Bred Versus American-Bred GSDs • The Basic Blueprint • German
Shepherd Dogs—White? • The Heart of the Matter: Dogs of Wisdom, Valor, and Skill

Chapter 3
PREPARING FOR YOUR GERMAN SHEPHERD DOG 41
Finding a German Shepherd Dog • Choosing the Right German Shepherd Dog for You •
Paperwork • Bringing Your New German Shepherd Dog Home • Supplies • Puppy-
Proofing Your Home • How to Keep Your German Shepherd Dog Happy • Travel

Chapter 4
FEEDING YOUR GERMAN SHEPHERD DOG 69
Diet Basics: Nutrients • Feeding Methods • Dog Food Labels • Types of Food •
Obesity

Chapter 5
GROOMING YOUR GERMAN SHEPHERD DOG 87
Grooming Supplies • Nail Care • Ear Care • Eye Care • Dental Care

Chapter 6
TRAINING AND BEHAVIOR OF YOUR GERMAN SHEPHERD DOG . 95
The Power of Positive Training • Socialization • Housetraining • Basic Training •
Formal Training • Problem Behaviors

Chapter 7
ADVANCED TRAINING AND ACTIVITIES
WITH YOUR GERMAN SHEPHERD DOG 127
The Canine Good Citizen® Program • Conformation • Formal Obedience •
Rally Obedience • Agility • Schutzhund Trials • Flyball • Skijoring • Herding •
Musical Freestyle • Service Dogs • Search and Rescue • Exercise, Games, and
Activities

Chapter 8
HEALTH OF YOUR GERMAN SHEPHERD DOG 145
Taking Your Dog to the Vet • Vaccinations • Parasites • Common Disorders and
Diseases • Canine Emergencies • Alternative and Complementary Medicine • The
Senior German Shepherd Dog

Resources 201

Index 203

HISTORY

of the German Shepherd Dog

The German Shepherd Dog (GSD) is the product of one man's intense and powerful vision. This man was Captain (Rittmeister) Max Emil Frederich von Stephanitz (1864-1936). His photo features a bald, grim-faced man with a firm mouth, trim white beard, ears a bit too large for his head, and compelling eyes. He is wearing his cavalry uniform with its neat row of ribbons, epaulets, and five-pointed star. What shines out unmistakably from the portrait, however, is an indomitable spirit, one that through some mysterious spiritual osmosis seemed to have been transmitted directly into the breed he helped to create.

Von Stephanitz's epiphany came on April 2, 1899, while attending the Karlsruhe Dog Show with his friend, Arthur Meyer. There he saw—and forthwith purchased—a four-year-old yellow and gray dog about 25 inches tall at the withers who possessed all of the qualities he believed essential in the perfect dog: intelligence, ability, weatherproof coat, and beauty. The dog was named Hektor Linksrhein, but von Stephanitz renamed the dog Horand von Grafrath. This began the trend toward using von within the German Shepherd Dog's name, which in Germany suggests a noble ancestry. This animal became the foundation dog of the German Shepherd Dog breed. (Another early dog, Roland von Starkenburg, the Grand Champion of 1906 and 1907, became the ancestor of most American German Shepherd Dogs.)

EARLY DEVELOPMENT OF THE BREED

It may come as a surprise to some that this noble and brilliant breed is a relative latecomer to the world of purebred dogs. Before von Stephanitz worked to develop the breed, German Shepherd Dogs were just that—dogs of various breeds belonging to German Shepherds and looking like nothing in particular and everything in general. These ancestors of the German Shepherd Dog resembled the modern version in a very vague way, but it was a hit-or-miss affair. Early breeders were interested only in function, not form, and while this appears to be a laudable practice, it actually brought about a lot of trouble. Many excellent sheepdogs were excellent despite rather

The stately and noble German Shepherd Dog is a relative latecomer to the world of purebred dogs.

than because of this body, and many passed on less than desirable genes to their offspring.

Von Stephanitz set out to explore what physical and mental characteristics went into a great dog. He became the cofounder and first president of the Verein für Deutsche Schäferhunde (club for German Shepherd Dogs), or simply the SV, founded in 1899, and he controlled and directed it with an iron fist. The first registered German Shepherd Dog was the aforementioned Horand von Grafrath, whose official number was SZ1. He appointed himself breeding master, judge, and breed inspector. "Beauty" itself meant nothing to him—he believed it naturally followed from form and utility. He even wrote for the standard description of the dog, "A

pleasing appearance is desirable, but it can not put the dog's working ability into question." The German Shepherd Dog standard was written to describe von Stephanitz's vision of the perfect, highly efficient herding dog. His maxim for the perfect dog became "Utility and Intelligence." As he wrote later, he sought a dog "...firm of nerve, attentiveness, unshockability, tractability, watchfulness, reliability, and incorruptibility together with courage, fighting tenacity, and hardness."

Having found what he believed to be the perfect male (Horand von Grafrath), von Stephanitz looked high and low for quality females to breed to him, searching all over Germany from Thuringia and Franconia to Wurttemberg. Thuringian and Franconian dogs tended to be wolf gray, wiry, and stocky in build, with erect ears and curled tails. Wurttemberg stock was larger and lop-eared, with excellent bones, straight tails, and good movement.

Obviously, a great deal of inbreeding was required to produce a breed that ran true to type. However, inbreeding reduces the gene pool and increases the risk of genetic diseases (compared to a large population of dogs who have bred randomly for generations). A balance had to be struck, and the result had to be not only the creation of excellent dogs, but dogs who bred "true to type," meaning that each generation would have the same basic characteristics as the first. Because von Stephanitz had served with the Veterinary College in Berlin, he brought some scientific expertise to this endeavor.

The Working German Shepherd Dog

Von Stephanitz was no fool, and he realized that as wonderful as the German Shepherd Dog was for his original job of sheepherding, this pastoral occupation was rapidly disappearing. The twentieth century would not be the golden age for shepherds. He also knew that unless a dog was bred for useful work, his native intelligence would suffer. As a result, von Stephanitz decided to invent an occupation for his beloved breed. He instituted programs in canine obedience, police work, and as a gesture to the breed's ancestry, herding trials. In order for SV club members to breed and register their dogs, von Stephanitz made it mandatory for breeders to demonstrate their dogs' ability to work. Consequently, a Schutzhund (protection dog) title was required, a title that has three parts: obedience, tracking, and protection. The

The Phylax Society

Even before von Stephanitz and his SV, a group of dog fanciers had formed the Phylax Society, a short-lived club intended to foster and standardize German breeds, primarily from the point of view of conformation. The club existed only from 1891 until 1894, but it provided the seed from which other breed clubs would later emerge.

Verein für Deutsche Schäferhunde also had conformation shows, known as Sieger, where the dogs would have to be rated G (good), SG (very good), V (excellent), or VA (excellent select), as well as have a hip certification to be allowed to breed. For a litter to be registered in Germany, both parents had to have working titles and at least a G (good) conformation rating.

Unbelievably, von Stephanitz at first had to literally beg German police departments to take a chance on his dogs. They laughed at him (probably making jokes about renegade sheep and so forth), but his perseverance eventually won them over, and the police soon found von Stephanitz's shepherd dogs to be invaluable law enforcement partners. Because of their all-around excellence, German Shepherds were in fact called "German Police Dogs" for many years. The German army found the breed invaluable as wartime messengers, guard dogs, and trackers, and the British and Americans, impressed despite themselves, began to take examples of the breed back home with them.

Redressing the Breed

Wisely, von Stephanitz was just as interested in deciding which dogs should not be bred, knowing that a few bad genes can ruin an entire breed. Von Stephanitz felt that his beloved breed was becoming too big and too square, with bad teeth and poor temperaments. In an attempt to redress the balance, in the 1925 Sieger show he chose as champion Klodo von Boxberg, a dog who was especially noted for his far-reaching gait. Klodo looked very

The first German Shepherd Dog show (Siegerschau) was held in 1899. The all-round male winner (Sieger) was a dog named Jorg von der Krone, and the female winner (Siegerin) was Lisie von Schwenningen.

different from many of the other dogs showing at the time, as he was set lower to the ground, appeared deeper and longer in body, and was shorter in the loin. This began the American taste for dogs with a sloping topline, very long croup, and extreme angulation characteristic of the breed in the United States today.

Klodo was imported to Maraldene Kennels in Hamden, Connecticut that same year; he proved to be a prepotent stud dog, and thus effectively introduced many of his unique qualities into the breed. Most contemporary German Shepherd Dogs in the United States can trace both their good and bad traits back to him.

The German Shepherd Dog was originally used for sheepherding; today, he participates in a variety of activities, including obedience, police work, and herding trials.

The Effects of World War I

After WWI, the German Shepherd's excellent qualities were so highly regarded (those were also the days of Rin Tin Tin and Strongheart) that breeders around the world went into a frenzy to

Helen Keller was an early owner of German Shepherds. Their connection with the visually impaired goes back many years.

import the dog. The result was the proliferation of badly bred creatures who were German Shepherd Dogs in name only. Puppy mills and fake pedigrees became the norm. Von Stephanitz understood the danger immediately, and he worked to create a Koerung (breed survey) that evaluated all dogs for breeding purposes and rejected from registration those dogs who failed.

Von Stephanitz was finally defeated, among other reasons, by the Nazis, many of whom were members of the SV. The Nazis pushed him out essentially by imposing their own rules, which no doubt were aimed more at promoting Hitler and themselves than with the good of the German Shepherd Dog. They essentially took over the club, and von Stephanitz, a broken man, gave up and quit in 1935. He died one year later, on April 22, 1936, the 37th anniversary of the founding of his beloved SV.

Rin Tin Tin and Strongheart

No history of the German Shepherd Dog would be complete without mention of Rin Tin Tin and Strongheart. The former, at least, was a real character. Toward the end of World War I, American Corporal Lee Duncan entered an exploded German bunker and found a mother (he later named her Betty) and a litter of five 10-day-old puppies. Duncan chose two of the puppies, a male and a female, while members of his battalion took the mother and the remainder of the pups back to their camp. (It turned out the litter came from prized Stephanitz lines.) Duncan named his puppies after tiny French puppets the children gave to the American soldiers for good luck, Rin Tin Tin and Nannette. Duncan then brought the two puppies home to America. Although Nanette died of pneumonia, the male grew up to become Rin Tin, Tin, a silent-movie star who managed to save Warner Brothers from financial disaster during the twenties. Starring in 26 films, he was most noted for his stunts (performed by himself, of course). At one time, Rin Tin Tin was the highest-paid "actor" in Hollywood, earning $1,000 a week. His life was reportedly insured for $100,000. Rinty died August 20, 1932 at the age of 14. He was laid to rest in a bronze casket, and his remains were later moved to Paris to a dog cemetery there. In 1997, Rin Tin Tin was inducted into the Pedigree Hall of Fame in the AKC's Museum of the Dog (St. Louis). There is still a Rin Tin Tin line. The current Rin Tin Tin VIII has his own agent, and Rin Tin Tin IX is waiting in the wings.

Another famous canine actor was Strongheart, whose real name was Etzel von Oringer, whelped in Germany in 1917. In 1920, he was brought to the United States by animal trainer Larry Trimble and writer Jane Murfin for the express purpose of making movies. While Strongheart had been carefully trained as an attack dog, his destiny apparently lay in Hollywood, where he enjoyed the good life as a pampered actor. His first movie was *The Silent Call*, and he went on to make many others, including, rather oddly, *White Fang*. Of course, Jack London's White Fang was half wolf and half dog, but a little makeup can work wonders. At any rate, Strongheart and his fellow star and mate Lady Jule were big sensations during the 1920s, and they attracted large crowds as they toured the country. Sadly, Strongheart fell against a hot studio light during the making of a film, and he later died from the injury.

Today, the SV continues to look after the welfare of this magnificent breed. It is the largest breed club in the world, having had 50,000 members and 600 branches at one time.

The Effects of World War II

World War II was a bad time for the German Shepherd Dog (as it was for just about everybody else). Thousands of dogs were slaughtered, and many family pets were confiscated by the army for military use. After the war, quality dogs were left, and malnutrition took its toll even on them. The entire stock had to be reinvented basically through the bloodlines of three sires: Rolf vom Osnabrücker-Land, Axel von der Deininghauserheide, and Hein vom Richterbach.

THE GERMAN SHEPHERD DOG IN THE UK

The German Shepherd Dog began to gain popularity in the UK after WWI when returning soldiers brought the dogs home with them. In 1919, the Kennel Club gave the breed a separate registry. In the beginning, only 54 individuals were listed, but by 1926, there were over 8,000. The anti-German phobia that was pervading England at the time caused a temporary name shift for the breed. It became known as the Alsatian Wolf Dog, a peculiar name that has actually stuck in some places. German Shepherd Dogs are, of course, no more closely related to wolves than Chihuahuas are, and calling this carefully bred sheepherding dog a "wolf dog" is far more prejudicial to the breed than was the original name. Finally, in 1977, the UK changed the name of the breed back to German Shepherd Dog, the name by which the breed is now known in the United States, Australia, and most other countries.

UK German Shepherd Dog Clubs

The British Association for German Shepherd Dogs (BAGSD) was formed in 1933, under the direction of Frank Riego. He held the job as Chairman of the club for 37 years. The first club was the "Birmingham and District Alsatian Club," Alsatian being the preferred name for the breed because of anti-German sentiment in the UK. In 1946, the name changed to the British Alsatian Association. Finally, in 1976, the Kennel Club decided to let

German Backlash

As had occurred in England, the United States went through its own period of anti-German frenzy during World War I. Dachshunds almost disappeared in the country, and even Beethoven's music passed under a cloud. Originally, the AKC had listed the breed under "German Sheepdog," even though the sponsoring club wished it to be called "German Shepherd Dog." During the war, however, the word "German" was dropped by both the AKC and the parent club. Unfortunately, many wonderful animals were actually destroyed by misguided "patriots."

Breed Registries

The American Kennel Club (AKC), founded in 1884, is the most influential dog club in the United States. The AKC is a "club of clubs," meaning that its members are other kennel clubs, not individual people. The AKC registers purebred dogs, supervises dog shows, and is concerned with all dog-related matters, including public education and legislation. It collects and publishes the official standards for all of its recognized breeds.

The United Kingdom version of the AKC is called the Kennel Club. However, the Kennel Club's members are individual persons. The membership of the Kennel Club is restricted to a maximum of 1,500 UK members in addition to 50 overseas members and a small number of honorary life members. The Kennel Club promotes responsible dog ownership and works on important issues like canine health.

bygones be bygones, and the breed regained its original name: the German Shepherd Dog.

At any rate, the organization, under the guidelines of the Kennel Club, had its first show in October 1934, with an entry of 120 German Shepherd Dogs.

In February 1968, Riego received a letter from the Director of the SV in Germany, proposing a meeting with all the leading German Shepherd Dog Clubs in Europe. The purpose of the meeting was to discuss the possibility of forming a European Union for the German Shepherd Dog.

A rival group, the German Shepherd Dog League of Great Britain, an older but smaller club, was also invited at this stage, but refused as it did not wish to be "dictated to" by a foreign country. The reason why both clubs were invited was because the League was the oldest club, but the BAGSD was the largest. The meeting took place on May 16th and 17th, 1968, at the SV office in Augsburg.

The BAGSD agreed with this unification but stated that in the UK, the Kennel Club controlled and ruled the organization of shows. It was also agreed that only countries recognized by the FCI would be permitted to join the union. The BAGSD was given the voting rights for the UK, as the English Kennel Club had a reciprocal agreement with the FCI, although it was not officially a member. In 1974, the umbrella organization was renamed the World Union for German Shepherd Dogs (WUSV). The BAGSD then helped the GSD League become an affiliated member to the WUSV, although the main delegate representing the UK was the BAGSD, and the voting system remained with them.

However, the United States and the UK still had a problem: Each has its own ruling body or Kennel Club. Recently, the WUSV has offered countries like the United Kingdom and US a 10-year period to conform to the regulations and practices required. The British organizations are working hard to make this happen, especially since they have been joined by the British Schutzhund Association, so that members dogs can pass their Begleithund (BH) test. A BH manual has been developed, as has a manual covering the breed standard and movement. It has been approved by both the Kennel Club and WUSV. The club holds an obedience championship show, two working trial championship shows, and several agility shows. In addition, the BAGSD and GSD League formed a small working party to share ideas to benefit the entire German Shepherd Dog community.

The German Shepherd Dog's name was temporarily changed to "Alsatian Wolf Dog" in response to pervading anti-German sentiment during the first half of the twentieth century.

Canadian GSDs

THE GERMAN SHEPHERD DOG COMES TO AMERICA

In 1908, the AKC registered its first German Shepherd Dog in the United States, a gray, black-saddled bitch named Queen of Switzerland, whelped on August 20, 1905 and owned by Adolph Vogt of Brooklyn. However, another dog called Mira of Dalmore (whelped in 1905) and shown as a "Belgium Sheepdog" (sic) was also probably a German Shepherd Dog of fine bloodlines. (Until 1912 or so, Belgian Sheepdogs and German Shepherd Dogs were shown in the same classes, although they were recognized as two distinct breeds.)

The breed was first registered in Canada in 1912. Established in 1922, the German Shepherd Dog Club of Canada, Inc. is the country's oldest active specialty breed club. It is also most likely the largest, with more than 500 members.

Hip Checks

In 1968, long before it became common in the United States, Germany began a program against hip dysplasia, radiographing the hips of thousands of dogs and recording the results. Dogs are given a Zuchtwert, or Hip Dysplasia Breed Value Assessment, based on the x-ray results from parents, siblings, and offspring.

During the German Shepherd Dog's early burst of popularity in America, quality fell behind quantity. As a result, health problems (like hip dysplasia, cataracts, elbow dysplasia, von Willebrand's disease, and epilepsy) and temperament problems (aggression) developed, as did (in show circles) misplaced regard for overangulation and other "showy" qualities that made the animal unfit for the work he was bred to do. Some of the trend toward showiness may be attributed to a German bitch named Flora Berkemeyer. Noted for her unusual grace and beauty, Flora helped make the German Shepherd Dog an acceptable show dog outside of Germany.

The German Shepherd Dog Club of America (GSDCA) was established in 1913 with 26 charter members. The first two conformation champions were awarded that same year—one to a dog named Luchs and one to a dog named Herta von Ehrengrund. One could say, however, that until 1917, "championships" were a rather hit-or-miss affair. For one thing, early judges knew practically nothing about the breed. For another, the early "point system" by which championships were awarded was geared to how many dogs were entered in an entire show rather than by breed, the way it is done today. There is no way of telling at this late date whether or not Lux or Herta were outstanding examples of the breed.

Another early show dog was Apollo von Hunenstein, a tan and gray dog whelped in Germany in 1912 and later imported to the United States, where he won his American conformation championship. While a well-known dog, many experts then and now considered him overrefined and even "bitchy," an adjective applied to a male dog who looks too feminine. His type was not particularly appreciated by American breeders, and he did not sire enough litters in the US to become a foundation stud. Nevertheless, he was respected enough to have his body stuffed, mounted, and presented to Yale's Peabody Museum when he died. That alone should give him a mention in history. It should also be noted that Apollo carried a recessive white gene that has caused a furor in recent years. The story of the white German Shepherd Dog is recounted in Chapter 2.

The GSDCA held its first specialty show in Greenwich, Connecticut in 1915, with an entry of 40 dogs. The first national German Shepherd Dog Specialty was held in 1918, and in 1925,

"Grand Victor" and "Grand Victrix" were designated as the top titles for the winners.

Influences

In addition to the aforementioned Klodo, another great influence on American German Shepherd Dogs was Sieger (Champion) Pfeffer von Bern, imported to the United States in 1936 to Hoheluft Kennels. He achieved Grand Victor status in 1937, returned briefly to Germany to win there, and then came back to the United States to win again.

Contemporary German Shepherd Dogs can trace their history to notable ancestors like Horand von Grafrath and Mira of Dalmore.

Another influence on American German Shepherds was Pfeffer (Pepper), a beautiful show dog who passed on many of his qualities to his offspring. However, he also introduced some faults into American lines, including a tendency toward missing teeth, overlong coats, overlong bodies, and temperament problems.

Another momentous 1950s import was Bernd von Kallengarten, a dog who introduced the solid black gene into American bloodlines. While Bernd had an excellent shoulder and forehand, bone, feet, suspension, head, croup, tailset, and body length, as well as a superior temperament, he also produced progeny with weak ears, steep croups, poor ligamentation, long coats, and a high percentage of hip and elbow dysplasia. I suppose you can't have everything, but this is an example where health may have been sacrificed for less important qualities.

Working Versus Show Dogs

In the United States, a split soon developed between old-style working German Shepherd Dogs and show stock, a split deplored by most lovers of this noble breed. From at least the 1950s, American breeders demonstrated a preference for a sloping topline and consequent severe rear angulation, as well as a very long loin. One dog who featured these qualities in abundance was Troll von Richterbach (ScH III, FH, ROM), 1957 Grand Victor (top dog at the national specialty). Troll was noted for his rear

German Shepherd Dogs from their native land have maintained uniformity in size, intelligence, and quality.

drive, hindquarter strength, muscle, bone, and gorgeous head. One of his famous litters (the so-called F litter) turned out six champions among the puppies. However, many of his later offspring had poor upper arms, weak ears, and blue or washed-out coloration.

German Shepherd Dogs are not the only breed to fall victim to differing ideas about what is desirable in a dog—almost all working and sporting breeds have been affected to a greater or lesser degree. To a lesser extent, the same has happened in some lines even in Germany now that Captain Max von Stephanitz is no longer with us. Most German breeders, however, have striven to maintain the standards set by the founder of the breed. Their results have paid off. German Shepherd Dogs from their native land have maintained a uniformity in size, intelligence, and quality that is unknown in the United States and the United Kingdom. *German* German Shepherd Dogs are still the most valued and sought after examples of the breed. Certainly most dogs used for working purposes, such as police dogs, do not come from American show stock but are imported from Europe at great expense.

Because the American and German types have become so divergent, crossbreeding between lines is not nearly as common as it was in earlier years. A few conscientious breeders, however, do keep the doors open and try to keep the German influence alive in American dogs.

Breeders of German Shepherd Dogs strive to maintain the athletic working ability of the breed.

Having said all this, I should say that all was not perfect in Germany. Many American breeders found von Stephanitz's program to be overly authoritarian, depriving breeders of the opportunities of using their own common sense and making their own decisions. They suggest von Stephanitz was a victim of many of the prejudices of his age, and his scientific theories—while fairly up to date for his time—are outmoded. Breeders in the US believe that American German Shepherds have their own place in the sun.

Chapter

2
CHARACTERISTICS
of the German Shepherd Dog

The German Shepherd Dog is currently one of the five most popular breeds both in the United States and the United Kingdom. One reason for the popularity of this breed is its extreme versatility—here is a dog who can indeed do anything and everything! However, increased popularity is a double-edged sword. While an undoubted compliment to the breed, it can also spawn careless breeding and unprincipled breeders who are in the "game" solely for the money.

Because of the extreme versatility of this breed, it has always been something of a conundrum as to how to classify the German Shepherd Dog for the purposes of dog show "groups." While it seems obvious from the name alone that the German Shepherd Dog should go into the Herding Group, that decision was rather late in coming. There's a practical reason for this—there was no Herding Group in the American Kennel Club until 1983. Before that time, the German Shepherd Dog was included in the Working Group, where he also fits, for he does all things with grace and aplomb. In the United Kingdom, the German Shepherd Dog is considered part of the Pastoral Group, which is simply a synonym for herding.

A good German Shepherd Dog has a harmonious structure, purity of line, and suppleness of movement. He is the perfect combination of power and agility. The GSD retains the natural proportions of his wolf-like ancestors and is mostly free of the arbitrary anatomical changes experienced by many other breeds.

TYPES OF GERMAN SHEPHERDS

While von Stephanitz wanted only a single type of German Shepherd—one who was a useful and hardworking dog as well as beautiful—his dream was doomed to disappointment. Only in Germany, where a dog must actually perform specific working tasks to attain a championship, has the breed retained its original look. In countries where conformation is judged in and of itself, that look began to change.

In the United Kingdom, the German Shepherd Dog is classed in the Pastoral Group, the UK's version of the AKC's Herding Group.

In the UK

In the UK, type suffered a serious "falling off" from the German standard. Compared to the German type, the English dogs were more angled in the hindquarter and had more prominent withers and sternums. Unfortunately, weak backs began to appear, reflecting poorly on the balance, strength, and harmony that is characteristic of this breed.

In fact, when Captain von Stephanitz himself took a turn judging dogs in England, way back in 1924, he was heard to remark, "It is good you English call these dogs Alsatians because they are definitely not German Shepherd Dogs."

Today, many breeders in the UK choose to still follow the German FCI standard, which is considered the blueprint for the breed. Others have selected for a heavier dog with a level topline.

In the US

The American GSD show dog is lighter and narrower, with a more refined head, a much greater extension at the trot, and more extreme angulation than his German counterpart, who seems almost chunky by comparison.

The change (or "downward slide" as many refer to it) toward the lighter-type dog began in the 1960s. Many people believe that the German-bred dog is sounder both temperamentally and physically than the American version. Some American aficionados of the breed maintain that the differences are slight and caused by language differences, although this seems unlikely. There are plenty of bilingual aficionados of this breed, and if language was the sole barrier, the same degree of differences would crop up in other breeds. Besides, in many breeds with similar standards and the same language, differences still arise.

Made in Germany

Many people believe that German Shepherd Dogs bred outside of Germany have lost much of their character and become timid, aggressive, or unstable. This problem has been avoided in Germany, where show and breeding stock (before the age of three and a half) must first pass through Schutzhund, a program that tests the dog's temperament and his ability to perform in tracking, obedience, and protection. He must also pass a Breed Survey, which includes an endurance test consisting of a 20-kilometer trot. All show GSDs in Germany must also pass a hip exam to ensure that they do not carry the genes for hip dysplasia. Offspring of highly qualified dogs receive a pink pedigree, while dogs of lesser ancestry receive a white one bordered in green.

THE BASIC BLUEPRINT

The criteria for the ideal German Shepherd Dog is presented in the breed standard, a written picture of the ideal GSD. In the United States, the standard was developed by the German Shepherd Dog Club of America. The United Kingdom has its own standard. There is another standard, however—the one written in Germany and used by the Fédération Cynologique Internationale (FCI), an organization devoted to promoting the development of purebred dogs (Germany was a founding member). While the organization has over 80 members, neither the United States nor the United Kingdom is a member, although both have working relationships with them. The FCI decides the country of origin for each breed, which in the case of the German Shepherd is Germany, of course. It then uses the standard of that country for its own. The German standard was last revised in 1991.

The German/FCI standard is a by-the-numbers work, compared with the more interpretative values written into the AKC or KC versions. For example, the FCI demands that the GSD's body should be 10 to 17 percent longer than the height, the neck should angle toward the head at 45 degrees, and so on. The KC merely says "slightly long in comparison to

The American GSD show dog is lighter and narrower than his German counterpart.

height," and the AKC is even vaguer—"longer than tall." There is currently a strong movement in the United States and in the United Kingdom to adopt the FCI standard verbatim, but as of this writing, it has not yet occurred. Australia has accepted the FCI standard as its own. In many respects, the standards are not dissimilar, although the interpretation of them by show ring judges and fanciers certainly has been.

The AKC standard was last revised in 1978 and reformatted in 1994; the most recent incarnation of the KC standard was in the year 2000. The main purpose of both standards is to inform breeders and exhibitors about the qualities that compose the perfect German Shepherd.

However, there is no "perfect" dog, and your GSD can be the best dog in the world (in your eyes), even if his eyes are too light or his nose is the wrong color. Eye and nose color, ear size, and tail carriage have no impact on a GSD's working ability.

I should note that German Shepherds often do not mature until they are two to two-and-a-half years old; obviously, younger dogs will not display the same level of perfection as older specimens. Here are a look at the breed standards. I have scattered a few German translations throughout the standard to give a feel for the breed's cultural background.

Fédération Cynologique Internationale

While many people have only heard of the American Kennel Club, Kennel Club, and perhaps some other national kennel clubs, an international organization actually exists. The Fédération Cynologique Internationale is the World Canine Organization, which includes 80 members and contract partners (one member per country), each of which issues its own pedigrees and trains its own judges. The founding nations were Germany, Austria, Belgium, France, and the Netherlands. It was first formed in 1911 but later disappeared during World War I. The organization was reconstituted in 1921. Currently, neither the United States nor Canada is a member.

The FCI ensures that its pedigrees and judges are recognized by all FCI members. Every member country conducts international shows as well as working trials; results are sent to the FCI office, where they are input into computers. When a dog has been awarded a certain number of awards, he can receive the title of International Beauty or Working Champion. These titles are confirmed by the FCI.

The FCI recognizes 331 dog breeds, and each of them is the "property" of a specific country, ideally the one in which the breed developed. The owner countries of the breeds write the standard of these breeds in cooperation with the Standards and Scientific Commissions of the FCI, and the translation and updating are carried out by the FCI.

In addition, via the national canine organization and the FCI, every breeder can ask for international protection of his or her kennel name.

Temperament

Temperament properly refers to the character of the dog. The German Shepherd is fearless but not hostile. He exudes self-confidence and a certain aloofness. He will stand his ground when strangers approach and accept kind overtures, although he is not overeager to make friends with new people. A shy, anxious, or aggressive dog is to be penalized. The AKC breed standard says that the GSD's character must be "incorruptible." The KC temperament section is briefer—it merely says that the dog is "steady of nerve, loyal, self-assured, courageous, and tractable."

Size *(Grösse)*, Proportion, and Substance

Size is always an important feature, as neither giant dogs nor miniature ones can possibly retain the other characteristics desired in this breed. The KC standard has the ideal height for males at 63

The breed standard of the German Shepherd Dog is a written picture of the ideal example of the dog.

Snow Nose

If you have a white German Shepherd Dog, his nose may turn lighter in the winter. This is called a "snow nose" and is harmless. Some people also believe a snow nose can result from eating or drinking from plastic dishes, but I haven't seen the evidence to support this theory.

cms (25 inches), and 58 cms (23 inches) for females. An inch (cm) either way is acceptable.

In the AKC standard, the desired height *(Höhe)* for males at the top of the highest point of the shoulder blade is 24 to 26 inches (61 to 66 cm) and for bitches, 22 to 24 inches (56 to 61 cm). Size is measured by taking a perpendicular line from the top of the shoulder blade to the ground. (Not including the hair, of course, so that may have to be pushed out of the way.) The FCI standard for dogs is 60 to 65 cm (23.5 to 25.5 inches) and for bitches 55 to 60 cm (21.5 to 23.5 inches), smaller than either of the others.

Unfortunately, a lot of novices to the breed go by the mistaken rule, "the bigger the better." This is definitely not true with German Shepherds. The standard is not looking for a giant-sized dog, but rather a strong *(kräftig)* and agile one. The GSD is longer than he is tall. (The ideal ratio has been given as 10:8.5, counting from the tip of the sternum to the back of the buttocks. It is very important not to confuse this total length with merely a long back, which is not desirable.) A square dog is not desirable in this breed, and neither is excessive height, which handicaps the desired trotting gait. Most show people try to accentuate this as much as possible by stretching the dog out with the right leg back. It looks a bit peculiar and does not fool the judge, but it is not discouraged, either.

Head *(Kopf)*

While the head of the GSD is an important element, it does not take precedence the way it does in some other breeds (such as the Bulldog). After all, a dog with a perfectly gorgeous head could be a disaster in the more important areas of substance, balance, and ability. The KC standard says the skull should be about 50 percent of the length of the overall head. The AKC standard calls for a noble, clean-chiseled head that has a masculine aspect in males and a distinctly feminine one in bitches. The KC standard doesn't mention nobility, nor does the FCI, although it agrees with the KC version of head length but in a slightly different form: The ratio of skull to muzzle is 50:50. The expression *(Ausdruck)* is keen, intelligent, and composed. The KC standard says the expression should be lively, intelligent, and self-assured. The FCI doesn't specifically address expression. The eyes are widely spaced, almond-shaped, and very dark *(dunkel)*. The ears *(Ohren)* are of generous size, moderately pointed, and are never cropped or hanging. Weak, soft, floppy ears are penalized. Some people believe the American version of the GSD has a narrower skull. Others maintain it is simply more refined.

The muzzle *(Nase)* is wedge-shaped, with only a slight "stop" where it meets the skull. The muzzle should not be "dish-faced" or "Roman" but parallel to the top surface of the skull. (A dish face is concave, while a Roman face is convex—both are faulty.) All three standards maintain that the nose must be black—any other color is cause for a disqualification.

According to the AKC standard, the German Shepherd's head should be noble, and his expression should be intelligent and composed.

It may seem odd that such a comparatively minor fault as an undesirable nose color would be enough to throw a dog out of the show ring, but that's the way it is. Fortunately, this kind of fault has no impact on the GSD's ability to make a terrific pet.

The jaws are strong, containing 42 teeth (the standard number for dogs), 20 on the top and 22 on the bottom. In the old days, German judges laboriously counted the teeth, but this is seldom done anymore. It is preferable for the dog to have complete dentition in both the AKC and KC standards. The FCI is more explicit, saying that the dentition "must be strong, healthy, and complete (42 teeth, in accordance with the dentition formula)." The quality of the bite, or the way the teeth and jaws come together, is extremely important in this hard-

working breed. The teeth must meet in a scissors bite, with the inner surface of the upper teeth touching and slightly protruding over the lower teeth. Dogs with a level bite (where the edges of the upper and lower teeth meet) are deficient, because a level bite can wear down teeth. A dog with an overshot *(oberschlachtig)* jaw is also penalized, but one whose jaw is undershot *(unterschlachtig)* (the lower jaw protruding beyond the upper on) is disqualified. An overshot jaw is more common, and although it is not as serious as an undershot jaw, it is nonetheless penalized.

Neck *(Hals)*, Topline, and Body

The neck is strong and muscular, clean-cut and relatively long, proportionate in size to the head, and without loose folds of skin. The FCI says that the skin should fit "loosely" but without forming folds. A relatively long, slightly crested neck is desirable, as it is indicative of power and strength. The head should be carried a bit forward rather than straight up.

The withers or shoulder blades are higher than the top of the shoulders, and they slope into a level (not roached or sagging) back. Any sag in the back is to be penalized. The back should be strongly developed and relatively short, and it should remain level while the dog is trotting.

The topline of the German Shepherd Dog is a major source of contention between German and American fanciers. The extreme sloping topline of the American GSD is disdained by German fanciers, while many German dogs have a roached "banana" back, which is usually accompanied by an incorrect croup. The KC standard says that "weak, soft, and roach backs" are undesirable and should be rejected. The topline should be "slightly sloping" from front to back.

The body (from point of the shoulders to rear of the buttocks) of the GSD is long. Again, the back *(Rucke)* itself is relatively short. The chest *(Brust)* is deep (at least to the level of the elbow in a mature dog) and spacious, with plenty of room for the lungs and heart. The ribs are well sprung, and they are wider and more widely spaced than those of some other breeds. If the ribbing is correct, the elbows *(Ellenbogen)* are able to move more freely. The abdomen should be firm and only moderately "tucked up." The loin is strong and of moderate length, and the croup *(Kruppe)* is quite long but not steep. It should form a gradual slope from the

pelvic bones to the set of the tail. (Dogs with too flat a croup carry their tails too high.)

The tail *(Rute)* is, of course, a continuation of the spine. It should be substantial and bushy and extend to the hock joint. This is the ideal length, but a longer tail is not considered faulty. The tail should be carried, in the inimitable language of the standard, "like a saber." The tail should have no kinks or curls in it.

A long, slightly crested neck is desirable in the German Shepherd Dog because it indicates power and strength.

Forequarters *(Vorderhand)*

The German Shepherd Dog is distinguished by his rather extreme angulation *(Winkelung)* (referring to the angle at which the joints meet), both in front and back. In the front, the shoulder angulation (where the upper arm meets the shoulder blade) should almost be at a right angle. This permits a very long step, which is desirable in the famous GSD trot. The shoulder blade itself is very long, with the shoulder sloping more in American dogs than is accepted by the German standard. The straighter shoulder encourages the head of the German-bred dog to be carried more forward than its American counterpart.

A continuation of the spine, the tail should be substantial, bushy, and extend to the hock joint, although a longer tail is not considered faulty.

The bones of the forelegs should be oval (not round). The forearm should drop straight to the pastern joint. The pasterns themselves are long and springy and angulated at about 25 degrees from the vertical. Many fanciers agree that the German-bred dogs have better pasterns (and feet) than the American-bred GSDs. Dewclaws may be removed or left on. (Most show dogs have them removed.)

The feet *(Photen)* are short and compact, with well-arched toes and short, dark nails. The pads should be thick and firm, and the feet should not turn inward or outward.

Hindquarters *(Hinterhand)*

Viewed from the side, there should be a right angle meeting of the upper and lower thigh. (The upper thigh is the counterpart in this instance to the shoulder blade.) The purpose of the rear angulation is to help the dog take a long and flexible stride. Excess angulation is too commonly seen in this breed, however. Technically, it's a fault called "saber hocks" and actually serves to weaken, not strengthen, the dog.

Rear dewclaws (which sometimes even come in pairs) are usually removed for English and American dogs; the FCI says nothing about their removal.

Coat *(Behaarung)*

The coat of the German Shepherd Dog comes in varying lengths and qualities; some standards around the world make provisions for these. In the United States, however, only one coat type is allowed: a medium-length double coat. The outer coat should be straight, harsh, and dense, lying close to the body. A slightly wavy or wiry coat is permissible. The undercoat is gray, slightly oily, and woollier than the outer coat, and it should not be visible to the naked eye.

The hair on the neck should be longer and thicker than that on the head, legs, or paws. Soft, silky, woolly, curly, or overlong coats are a fault.

The Kennel Club is more lenient in the matter of hair length, stating only that "no hard and fast rule for length of hair exists. The length is truly variable, and many "intermediate" forms exist. The "normal" stock (short) coat is very thick with straight individual hairs that are straight, coarse, and lying flat against the body. The hair is usually short on the head (including the ears), as well as on the front of the legs and toes. It's longer on the neck and back of the legs (as far as the pastern and hock joint), so it looks almost as if the dog is wearing short pants. A slightly heavier version of this coat is sometimes called a "plush" coat and is seen frequently in German show rings.

The outer coat of the German Shepherd Dog should be straight, harsh, and dense.

A longer "stock" coat has hairs that may not lie close to the body, and the coat is longer around the ears, back or forearm, and in the loin region. Sometimes the ears will have tufts. Many breeders consider this type of coat undesirable, as it lacks some of the waterproofing quality of the normal stock coat. However, this coat does have a good undercoat.

There is also a GSD coat that is actually "long." It tends to be soft, wavy, and forms a part along the back. Its waterproofing quality is poor, and it's not considered desirable. This type of coat also does not have an undercoat and so provides insufficient warmth. Some people who see these dogs mistake them for a cross between a Collie and a GSD! A long coat is a disqualifying fault for the FCI.

The distinctive gait of the German Shepherd is elastic and outreaching.

This breed sheds all year round! If you can't stand the idea of hair blowing all over the place, consider another breed or be assiduous in your grooming.

Colors *(Farbe)*

The German Shepherd Dog varies in color, and most colors are permissible, including solid black *(tiefschwarz)*, although this color is not usually preferred in the United States. (Most solid black dogs have a few tan hairs between the toes and in the rectal area. anyway.) The KC standard wisely says that "color in itself is of secondary importance having no effect on character or fitness for work." However, it does prefer black or black saddle with tan, or gold to light gray markings. Blues, livers, albinos, whites, and near whites are considered undesirable. The FCI says sternly, "The color white is not permitted." (It's rather well known that von Stephanitz didn't like white dogs.) The FCI permits black with reddish tan,

tan, gold to light grey markings, all black, and all grey; in greys with dark shadings, black saddle and mask.

Most German Shepherd Dogs come in some variety of black and tan, usually with a black mask. Strong, rich colors are preferred, and they are found more often in European dogs. In addition, German-bred dogs tend to have a more uniform coloring, often a dark mahogany with a black saddle. Pale, washed-out colors and blues or livers are serious faults.

A white dog must be disqualified in AKC conformation shows. A small bit of white on the chest is permitted but not preferred. "Tan" is interpreted as any shade of brown, from fawn or even silver to deep mahogany. The amount of tan is also quite variable. The color called "sable," a variety of agouti, the wild wolf color, is the most popular in the United States. Sable-colored dogs have banded guard hairs tipped with black. Agouti comes in several varieties, such as golden, gray, or mahogany, depending on which color is predominant.

The GSD in Motion

The movement of the German Shepherd Dog is distinctive. He is considered a trotting dog, whose hind foot and fore foot on opposite sides move simultaneously in a long, outreaching motion. The gait is best observed from a distance.

Gait (Gang)

Gait refers to the way the dog moves and is more important in the standards of GSDs than in almost any other breed.

The German Shepherd Dog is a trotting dog. The trot is a diagonal movement in which the hind foot and the forefoot on opposite sides move simultaneously. (It's easier observed than described. The gait is best observed at a medium-fast pace, with the observer a fair distance away.) This movement is extremely important in considering the overall quality of the dog.

The gait is long, flexible, elastic, and outreaching. The feet travel close to the ground, and the hindquarters deliver a powerful forward thrust that drives the body forward. For the smoothest stride, the forequarters and hindquarters must be similarly proportioned and angulated. Dogs who are overangulated in the rear and underligamented in general have diminished soundness, no matter how faddish this trend is. In fact, it is becoming quite difficult to find good dogs without this overangulation in the United States. (Many European dogs, on the other hand, are underangulated in the front.)

While the gait of the German Shepherd Dog is sometimes referred to as "floating," this is wrong and not referred to in any breed standard. However, this is the style of movement that has

It is interesting to compare the GSD's standards from different countries.

become popular with some exhibitors, judges, and spectators, albeit to the detriment of the breed.

Disqualifications

US

- Cropped or hanging ears.
- Dogs with noses not predominantly black.
- Undershot jaw.
- Docked tail.
- White dogs.
- Any dog who attempts to bite the judge.

FCI

- Weak character, savageness or nervousness.
- Proven "severe H.D" (hip dysplasia).
- Monorchids and cryptorchids, as well as dogs with clearly uneven or atrophied (stunted) testicles.
- Disfiguring ear or tail defects.
- Deformities.
- Dentition faults, missing:
- 1 Pre-Molar 3, and one further tooth, OR 1 Canine, OR 1 Pre-Molar 4, OR 1 Molar 1 OR 1 Molar 2 OR 3 or more teeth altogether.
- Jaw defects: Overshot 2mm or more. Undershot. Level bite in the whole region of the incisors.
- More than 1cm over or under size.
- Albinism.
- White coat colour (even with dark eyes and nails).
- Long double coat (Long Stockhaar): Long, wavy, topcoat not lying closely, with undercoat, feathering on ears and legs, bushy breeches and bushy tail forming flags below.
- Longcoat: Long, soft top coat without undercoat, usually with a parting down the back, flags on ears and legs and tail.

UK

According to the breed standard, "Any departure from the foregoing points should be considered a fault and the seriousness with which the fault should be regarded should be in exact proportion to its degree and its effect upon the health and welfare of the dog."

GERMAN SHEPHERD DOGS —WHITE?

Probably nothing has caused more controversy in the German Shepherd Dog world as the argument over white dogs. Occasionally, a German Shepherd Dog will be born white. This is not a rare thing at all. In fact, over 5,000 white GSDs are registered with the American Kennel Club every year. The white gene has been around from the beginning of the breed. As we saw earlier, the first registered German Shepherd Dog was Horand von Grafrath, whose maternal grandfather was a white dog named Grief. Thus, the white gene has been present in GSDs since the breed's inception. In 1921, von Stephanitz published a book on the German Shepherd Dog that included a photo of a celebrated white German Shepherd Dog, Berno v.d., who was a direct descendant of Hektor. Some of the best early German lines, such as V. Oeringen, Strongheart, Rin Tin Tin, and Long Worth bloodlines frequently produced white dogs.

Some people have always had a penchant for white German Shepherds. The Royal House of Hapsburg dabbled in them, ostensibly because the Queen wanted a white dog to match her

Although there has been much controversy regarding white German Shepherd Dogs, they are popular and beloved pets.

The White Debate

There seems to be no evidence that white is associated with deafness in German Shepherds, as it is in some other breeds. Nor is a white German Shepherd an albino, which is indeed associated with many health concerns. In fact, there is some evidence that white German Shepherd dogs may be freer of certain genetic conditions than are some standard-colored dogs. On the other hand, breed clubs have long maintained their right to establish standards based upon mere preferences, and many breed standards contain lists of disqualifying colors. There doesn't seem to be a "right" or "wrong" on this issue, which probably accounts for much of the debate.

white dresses and white Lipizzaner horses. Ann Tracy, who owned one of the first two German Shepherd champions on record in the United States, imported some excellent show stock from Germany, and white puppies immediately appeared in her litters. In the United States, the first registered white GSDs were whelped from Tracy's stock on March 27, 1917: Stonihurst Edmund, Stonihurst Eric, Stonihurst Eadred, and Stonihurst Elf.

White is a recessive gene that can be "hidden" for many generations before making an appearance. Both parents must carry the gene to produce white puppies, and mated white individuals will always produce white offspring. A white dog bred to a dog who does not carry the gene, however, will not produce white puppies.

The Campaign Against White German Shepherd Dogs

The campaign against white German Shepherd Dogs began in Germany. Whites were erroneously blamed for various genetic problems that began showing up in the breed; they were also blamed for "fading color" (never desirable). There is no truth to either of these allegations, but white puppies born in Germany were drowned and their birth records destroyed.

In 1968, following Germany's lead, white became a disqualifying fault for German Shepherd conformation in the AKC standard (which is derived from the German Shepherd Dog Club of America), although these dogs are eligible for registry with both the American Kennel Club and United Kennel Club. In 1980, the Canadian Kennel Club was petitioned by the German Shepherd Dog Club of Canada to disqualify white GSDs from the conformation show ring. They got their way, and currently, white German Shepherd Dogs cannot compete in CKC conformation competition, although there was a hard fight over this change. As in the AKC, whites can participate in tracking, herding and other performance events.

White GSDs are disqualified from the show ring in part, the AKC states, because a white dog would not be visible to a shepherd—he would blend in with the sheep, which makes a certain amount of sense. However, white German Shepherd Dogs are eligible for AKC-sanctioned herding trials, which seems, at least on the surface, slightly contradictory. I should also mention that it is said with equal fervor on the other side that white is a desirable characteristic in a sheepdog, because it enables the shepherd to tell the dog from a wolf at a distance. (European wolves are not usually white.) White German Shepherds are eligible for other AKC events besides herding, including obedience, tracking, and agility, and they excel at all of them.

Showing the White German Shepherd Dog

White GSDs can be exhibited at many rare breed shows (although they are not particularly rare) and are also eligible to earn conformation titles with some other kennel clubs, such as the United Kennel Club.

Admirers of the white German Shepherd Dog (mostly in the United States, Canada, and Switzerland) also began to breed them. In 1964, fanciers in Sacramento, California formed the first White German Shepherd Dog Club. Some breeders of these white dogs believe that they are simply continuing to breed the white variety of German Shepherd Dog. Others believe that the breed has evolved somewhat separately and should be considered a new breed and compete separately in the show ring. This is how it is done in many

White German Shepherd Dogs are the beloved companions of those who share their lives, whether as simply pets or as show dogs.

European countries, as the white variety is not accepted in conformation by any European German Shepherd breed clubs or by the FCI. The United Kennel Club will accept white German Shepherd Dogs in conformation, where they compete against standard German Shepherds of other colors.

White GSDs in the UK

White GSDs do occur in the United Kingdom as well. They can be recognized by the Kennel Club under the name German Shepherd Dog (Alsatian); however, this color is not acceptable for the show ring. This seems to be a domino effect from the disqualification of dogs of this color in the show ring by the German Shepherd Dog Club of America in 1968.

The White and Long Coat Shepherd Society was established in 1985. It has members throughout the UK, France, Germany, and Australia. There are also White Shepherd clubs in Sweden, Denmark, Canada, and Holland. Again, white is a naturally occurring color for this breed—the White German Shepherd is not an albino. Albinos have no pigmentation, but the White German Shepherd has black pigmentation on his nose, eye rims, paws, and around his mouth. They do not have any more health or temperament problems than their darker cousins.

Both white and long-haired dogs are used by police, military, and prison services. They serve as guide dogs for the blind and are also used as therapy dogs.

THE HEART OF THE MATTER: DOGS OF WISDOM, VALOR, AND SKILL

The official breed standard can only touch on the magic of this iconic dog. Tireless heroes, wise guides to the blind, guardians of the home, and working sheepdogs, German Shepherd Dogs are indubitably one of the most versatile, all-around "can-do" breeds in existence today.

Strong, enduring, intelligent, and discriminating, the German Shepherd Dog is truly an elite animal. He is known for his elegance, glamour, discipline, and intelligence. Wary of strangers, this dog will make you earn his love. Once his heart is won, though, the German Shepherd Dog is a friend for life. He is also quick to defend those he loves.

German Shepherds enjoy being near their families and do not tolerate being left alone for long periods of time. They require early training, training that is loving and firm. They do not respond well to anger, coercion, or violence.

More than most other breeds, the German Shepherd Dog has suffered from a surfeit of irresponsible breeding. The well-bred GSD, though, is simply one of the world's best dogs—steady, reliable, intelligent, tolerant, and faithful. Ill-bred types can be neurotic and even dangerous.

Temperament

This is a dog who needs work to be happy. Little is beyond his ability, but he is definitely not a couch potato! The GSD needs a job, and if he is not given one, he can become destructive and neurotic.

Housing and Exercise Requirements

The German Shepherd Dog is an extremely active dog, and he does best in a large house with plenty of room. That doesn't mean you can't keep one in an apartment, but it does mean that apartment dwellers need to be extra conscientious about exercising their GSDs, as they will become bored and destructive if underexercised. Of course, if you're in love with the breed but aren't too crazy about running for miles every day, please consider adopting a senior dog—you'll get all of the magic without the marathons.

Trainability

The German Shepherd Dog is both extremely intelligent and highly trainable. That's why he is so widely used in police work, service work, the military, and in fact almost any occupation you can think of. However, the German Shepherd Dog has a streak of independence that makes him smart enough not to obey meaningless commands. He responds best to careful, consistent training that has a goal. These dogs are particularly adept at problem solving.

Although German Shepherds can live in an apartment, they do best in large houses with plenty of room.

Grooming

While the German Shepherd Dog is not as difficult to groom as a Poodle, this breed does shed a lot, and sheds all year round. In addition, longer-coated German Shepherds tend to blow their coats in the spring and fall, which can really line your house with fur. Regular brushing at least three times a week will help keep this coat under control.

Bonding

German Shepherd Dogs will bond to the entire family, and they are normally excellent with and protective of the family children. However, because of the strength and power of this breed, children and pups need to be well supervised and socialized toward each other. And remember, because this breed's original function was as a herding dog, expect that your kids may sometimes be "herded" as well.

Other Pets

Most German Shepherds are tolerant of other family pets, although I have known a few who really disliked cats. Most of the time, though, they are kind and accepting of other dogs.

Protection Ability

The German Shepherd Dog is one of the best protection dogs there is. He is territorial and will guard your home and family and fight to the death if threatened. Interestingly, GSDs soon learn who is in the "magic circle" and who is not. My next-door neighbors rent an apartment in the back of their home, and their GDSs are introduced to each new tenant. Immediately after the introduction, the tenants are not only free to come and go as they please, but they are included in the protective circle of the family itself. The main worry about this breed is not that the dog may be protective, but that he may be overprotective.

German Shepherd Dogs are usually protective of the children in their family.

Self-Sufficiency

While German Shepherds are smart, independent thinkers, they are not crazy about being left alone for extended periods of time. They don't suffer to any extraordinary degree from separation anxiety, but they really thrive when they are in close contact from their owners.

Life-Saving German Shepherd Dogs

German Shepherd Dogs can and have done it all. Most famously, they are courageous police dogs. One such dog, Robo, received a posthumously awarded Medal of Valor from the North American Police Work Dog Association. Other GSDs participate in search and rescue, like Sam, who works with his handler, Guenther Findling, with the Red Cross in Germany. Trained to find missing persons, he barks an alert and remains with the person until his handler arrives.

One special German Shepherd service dog named Ben saved his owner's life in a creative way. His owner, Karen, had returned home from open heart surgery. A bad drug combination had resulted in her losing consciousness and experiencing severe respiratory distress. Although Ben had not been trained to dial 911 (some helper dogs are), he was on hand when the phone rang. It was Karen's father calling to check up on her. Ben managed to lift the receiver out of the cradle, and he proceeded to bark furiously into it after carrying the phone close to Karen so that her dad could hear her labored breathing. Karen's father called the paramedics, and when they arrived a few minutes later, they stared warily at the large, protective animal. Ben, however, immediately ceased barking, quietly backed out of the room, and sat down in the kitchen, allowing the medics to do their job—saving Karen's life. And they did—with just a little help from her best friend!

The German Shepherd Dog matches nobility of character with natural beauty of form. Not for a weak or neglectful owner, this breed will honor his family with lots of loyalty and a strong protective instinct. To ensure that this is the right breed for you, you'll need to look beyond the myth and outward elegance of the German Shepherd Dog to the incredible dog within. The next chapter will help you do just that.

Because German Shepherds are so intelligent and trainable, they are often used in police work.

3

PREPARING

for Your German Shepherd Dog

We are not born into the world ready to receive a German Shepherd Dog into our lives. This momentous occurrence takes planning, an effort that includes evaluating your needs, your ability to care for a dog, household space, finances, and psychological readiness of you and other family members to care for a dog. Many people simply underestimate how much time, money, and care a dog really requires, which results in dogs simply not being cared for properly. Don't even consider getting a German Shepherd Dog unless you are willing to commit to a lifetime partnership with this intelligent and affectionate animal.

FINDING A GERMAN SHEPHERD DOG

German Shepherds come in two varieties: immature (puppy) and mature (dog). All dogs start as puppies, and all puppies turn into dogs. Most people, especially most first-time dog owners, want a puppy. And puppies are wonderful! They are warm, cuddly, and extremely irresistible. Choosing a puppy has several other advantages, too. You get to train your dog right from the beginning, and you don't have to deal with the training mistakes made by former owners. If you get your pup from a good breeder, you'll most likely have a healthy and psychologically sound dog as well.

Puppies aren't for everyone, though, and while they are charming and undeniably cute, there are many reasons to consider getting an older dog. One obvious reason is appearance. A puppy, even from a reputable breeder, is always something of an unknown quantity. An adult dog, on the other hand, is there in all his size and glory. Older dogs are usually housetrained, and they have finished with the disastrous chewing stage. And despite the old adage, old dogs can learn, and they learn quickly. In fact, they have a longer attention span and are less likely to be distracted than puppies. Additionally, older dogs are often well-socialized and understand how to get along with others—something many puppies still have to experience. Older dogs are loving and grateful to have a good home. Although German Shepherd Dogs have the reputation of being one-person or one-family dogs, they adjust quite quickly to new situations. If they didn't, the police and other authorities would be out of luck

The decision whether to own a puppy or adult German Shepherd Dog is one that requires a good deal of thought and research.

acquiring a trained dog! Older dogs need less supervision than puppies, and they are instantly ready to join you on long walks and other grown-up activities. And they won't keep you awake all night crying for their mothers.

Of course, there's a downside to everything. Many older dogs are given up because of temperament or training problems, so it's important to be sure you know the whole story before you decide to adopt an older dog.

Finally, whether you choose a male or female German Shepherd Dog is a matter of personal preference. If you already have a dog, it's often wise to choose a second dog of the opposite sex, but there's no hard and fast rule about this. Neither are there any real character differences between male and female dogs. (By the way, unless you are showing your dog, you should have both sexes neutered.)

Breeders

Breeder Pros and Cons

If you plan to show or work your German Shepherd, your source should be a responsible breeder. Breeders specialize in raising GSDs with specific goals in mind, and if you share those goals, there's no better place to get a dog. To find a reputable breeder, contact your local all-breed kennel or German Shepherd club; they can point you in the right direction.

The biggest disadvantage of breeders is finding the right one. Many people pose as reputable breeders but aren't, which is why the advice of your local kennel club is so important. Reputable breeders are also quite choosy about prospective owners, and with good reason. The German Shepherd Dog needs a special kind of owner, and it's the breeder's job to make sure you fill the bill.

Selecting a Breeder

If you are interested in showing your dog or participating in competitive events, your best chance of success is to buy a puppy from a responsible breeder. More so than in almost any other breed, many German Shepherd Dog breeders "specialize." They may concentrate on breeding companion animals, therapy dogs, or breeding for conformation or performance (in areas like Schutzhund, obedience, or herding). Be sure you decide what kind of GSD you are looking for, and match your needs with a breeder

Insurance Targets

According to the Centers for Disease Control, the German Shepherd Dog is the breed third most likely (after "Pit Bull types" and Rottweilers) to be targeted by home insurance companies for restricted coverage.

After you have found the right breeder, ask for her help in selecting the right puppy for you and your family.

who can supply them. Your local all-breed kennel club can help put you in touch with the kind of breeder you need.

After You've Selected a Breeder

Once you find the right breeder, allow her to guide you in selecting the perfect puppy for your family. After all, the breeder knows her dogs better than anyone else. In fact, many good breeders write down their observations about each puppy in a notebook. For example, some pups are extroverts, while others are reserved. Some enjoy wrestling and playing, while others enjoy cuddling more. These different preferences suggest different temperaments.

When visiting, bring the entire family. Everyone should have an investment in this puppy. If you have young children, the breeder will want to watch them interact with the puppies. She may also be interested in seeing how much control you have over your own kids.

The breeder will ask you many questions. Her main interest is not making money (and you'd be surprised to see how little good breeders make on selling a dog), but improving the breed and finding the right homes for her puppies. She may ask you questions about your lifestyle, your expectations, and your knowledge of the breed. The key is to be completely honest with the breeder about your intentions. If you are seriously interested in Schutzhund or agility work, say so. If your interests lie more toward a protector or companion or show dog, tell her that. Breeders are not mind readers, and they can help you make appropriate choices only if you give them enough information to allow them to do so.

Pay special attention to the temperament of the mother dog (dam). This is the temperament that will most likely be passed onto the puppies. You may also want to look at other dogs owned by this breeder to check out their temperaments, as well. Good breeders are proud of the dogs they produce and should be happy to show them to you.

You, too, should have some questions for the breeder. These might include:

- What was the goal of breeding this litter?
- What events have the parents competed in, and what titles have they earned?
- Is there a photograph of the sire available if he is not on the premises?

Pet Preferred

If you're not planning on showing and you are dealing with a breeder who specializes in conformation, explain that you are looking for a "pet-quality" GSD. This doesn't mean there will be anything at all wrong with the puppy. It just means that in the breeder's opinion, the puppy will not achieve a championship in the show ring. Eyes that are too light, a nose that is the wrong color, or weak ears are just a few unimportant factors that may limit a dog's "show worthiness" but have no effect on his ability to make a great companion for you and your family.

- What health clearances do the parents and grandparents have? (You should be especially interested in hip and elbow dysplasia, which are common in GSDs.)
- Have the puppies visited the vet for their first health check?
- What health guarantees come with the puppy?

Breeders who cannot answer these questions to your satisfaction should be passed over.

Rescues and Shelters

Rescue and Shelter Pros and Cons

Adopting a dog from a shelter or rescue makes a real, tangible difference in more lives than you can imagine. First of all, every shelter, every pound, and every rescue group in the country is full. Every day, thousands of dogs are put to sleep—not because they are ill or vicious, but because there is simply no more room for them. Few dogs who go to the shelter will find homes, and every 6.7 seconds a dog is euthanized. Rescue groups have better success, but most are too small to take in large numbers of dogs. When you accept a shelter/rescue dog into your home, you are making room for another dog who may now have a chance at life. You've saved two dogs!

Dogs are given up to rescues and shelters for various reasons. Sometimes a dog's former owner dies. Sometimes a dog is found as a stray or collected because of owner abuse. Sometimes people decide they no longer want their dog for a variety of reasons. Just because a dog has been put in a rescue or shelter does not necessarily mean that you can adopt one for free, however. Rescue groups depend on donations and backbreaking fundraisers. Many of the dogs they receive require extensive medical care, usually due to mistreatment or neglect.

Adopting a German Shepherd Dog from a rescue or shelter will make a tangible difference in his life.

However, your cost to adopt will be considerably less than the cost of buying a puppy from a breeder.

Along with the love you'll receive from your adopted GSD, you can also expect some problems. With a rescue or shelter dog, many of the problems revolve around trust issues. He has been abandoned at least once before, and he may be slow to give his heart for fear of it being broken—again. Rescue or shelter dogs also often come with serious psychological baggage, which is no surprise. Even a well-cared-for dog who has been loved in the past may be terribly unhappy and disoriented. He probably misses his old home and doesn't understand why he has been given up. This can lead to a multitude of problem behaviors, like dominance issues, shyness, chewing, obsessive-compulsive behavior, excessive barking, poor health, and most frequently, separation anxiety. Rescue dogs require particular compassion and understanding, as these concerns will not magically disappear.

A good rescue or shelter should be very knowledgeable about German Shepherd Dogs.

Although they have been "dumped," rescue and shelter dogs are not garbage. Some even shine in competition! Many adopted dogs have gone on to earn performance titles or excel at therapy work. And while it's true that many adopted dogs come with "baggage," kind treatment and patience usually work wonders. Dogs are much more flexible than people, and with loving care, most manage to forget their gloomy pasts.

The difference you'll make in your new dog's life will be immeasurable. You may be providing your rescue dog's first toy, bed, and love. You may be taking him for his first walk, his first romp, or his first visit to the vet. You may be giving him the first kind words he's ever heard. However, the biggest difference will be in your own life. The feeling of having saved a life will enhance and enrich your own. The love you get from a previously unloved and unwanted dog easily matches any facile puppy devotion. Luckily, GSDs combine the qualities of loyalty and adaptability; your new dog will not "pine away" for his former owners, most of whom neglected him. He will transfer his abiding affection to you, who will be well worthy of it!

Older dogs who need homes can make wonderful companions—and they're usually trained!

Selecting a Rescue or Shelter

Choosing a responsible shelter or rescue is a lot like choosing a breeder. A good rescue or shelter will ask you a lot of questions, will know its dogs and the breed overall backward and forward, and will be available to help you during the adjustment period. A good shelter or rescue will also agree to take the dog back if a problem occurs. Obviously, they can't guarantee the behavior of their charges 100 percent, but a good rescue or shelter will perform temperament testing and keep the dog in a foster home for a period of time before adoption so that his temperament can be evaluated.

After You've Selected a Rescue or Shelter

A reliable rescue issues a contract the same way a good breeder does. Nearly all rescue groups stipulate that if the dog doesn't suit or can't adapt to your family, you will return him to the rescue, not resell him or give him away. Most rescues also require a home visit and vet check before they will allow you to adopt one of their dogs. The dogs they deal with have already been traumatized; rescue groups want to make sure that the new home will be the last one.

Healthy puppies should appear clean, happy, and active. They are all cute, so let the breeder's knowlege of their individual temperaments guide your selection.

Pet Stores

Some people decide to buy a German Shepherd Dog from a pet store. Pet stores can be a convenient option, and they usually offer a wide selection of puppies. It is important to remember, though, that a dog's health, happiness, and well-being are largely dependent on his genetics and the quality of his early care. This is why you must ask the pet store to provide you with all the details of the German Shepherd Dog's breeding and history. In fact, pet store employees should be knowledgeable about dogs in general and the breeds they sell in particular.

If you are considering a GSD from a pet store, check the dog for any signs of poor health. A few signs of illness are nasal discharge, watery eyes, and diarrhea. A store should not be selling a dog experiencing any of these symptoms. Even if the puppy seems healthy, be sure to have him checked by your veterinarian as soon as possible. Many health guarantees offered by pet stores are contingent upon a veterinary examination within a few days of the sale.

CHOOSING THE RIGHT GERMAN SHEPHERD DOG FOR YOU

Like people, German Shepherd Dogs are individuals. Each has his own looks and character. Being able to match the individual dog to the perfect owner is sometimes difficult, but you can often facilitate the process through careful observation.

Physical Appearance

Great puppies (and adults) have a clean look and smell, are friendly and of an appropriate weight, without a pot belly, which can be a sign of worms. Beware of puppies with chewed up or missing fur, distressed breathing, lethargy, diarrhea (or a dirty rear end), discharge from the nose or eyes, or a wobbly, uneven gait.

Temperament

Watch the puppies move. While you can't tell too much at this stage, a well-moving puppy is a good sign. Pick up the puppy of your choice and cradle him on his back in your arms, just the way you'd hold a baby. It is best to sit on the floor for complete security. He may struggle a bit and that's okay, but a real fighter may be too independent to be the ideal family pet. As you hold him, see if he makes eye contact with you. A dog who won't make eye contact may grow up to be too timid. The adult GSD should have many of these same characteristics. Overall, he should be friendly and confident, with no trace of viciousness or shyness.

The breeder may have done a temperament test on the litter and will be glad to share the results, but I have some doubts about their efficacy. If performed at the wrong time (even by a day or so, according to some authorities) or by the wrong person in the wrong way, they will yield little information. Your best bet is to observe the puppies yourself. How do they react to each other? To strangers? To their breeder? A good puppy is friendly and not too independent, but he is not shy, either. He should explore his surroundings but also enjoy being held and comforted. If he falls asleep in your arms, that's not a bad thing!

A puppy with a good temperament will be friendly, and he should not appear too independent or too shy.

Allow the breeder to help you select the right dog. She's been observing you while you have been observing the puppy. At this point, she should know about you, your family, your lifestyle, and your goals, and she probably has an idea of what pup will work

best in your home. It helps if you know your own mind as well. Are you looking for a pet, a hunt prospect, or a show dog? Are you interested in obedience, agility, or just wandering around the dog park? Be as honest as possible, and you'll end up with a better dog for your home.

PAPERWORK

Although buying a puppy is a highly emotional experience, it's also a business deal. You should receive a contract that states what puppy you are buying, his birth date, price, the registered names and numbers of both parents, and the names and contact information for both breeder and buyer.

Neutered dogs can't be shown in conformation, although they can compete in obedience and other events.

The contract will also state when you will receive the application for registration so that you can register your dog. If you have a spay/neuter agreement (often the case with a pet-quality, as opposed to a show-quality, pup), that will also be in the contract. With this type of agreement, the breeder may also choose to give you a "limited registration," which means that if you don't hold up your end of the deal and neuter your dog, the puppy won't be eligible for registration. Limited registration can be changed to open registration at any time. This sometimes occurs if the puppy suddenly demonstrates show-dog promise.

Make sure that all guarantees the breeder gives are in writing. These guarantees may refer to present or future medical conditions, such as hip dysplasia. Hips cannot be certified until after the dog is two years old. The acceptable "grade" of the hips should also be included in the contract.

You should receive a medical record for the puppy that indicates the veterinary care he has received, including deworming, vaccinations, and physical exams. You should also receive a feeding schedule that sets forth the amount and type of food your puppy has been eating. Finally, the breeder should give you a two- to three-day supply of food and a towel or toy the puppy is familiar with to help ease his transition to your home.

If possible, you should take your puppy to see your own vet within 48 hours of purchase, especially if the contract has a clause that allows you to bring the puppy back if your vet determines he is not in good health. The contract should also say how the situation will be remedied.

Don't forget to have the contract signed by all concerned! A

If your puppy is engaging in an undesirable behavior, such as chewing your shoelaces, offer him a replacement item.

good breeder will keep in touch with you about how the puppy is doing and help resolve any problems.

BRINGING YOUR NEW GERMAN SHEPHERD DOG HOME

Bringing your new dog home is a thrilling event! Although you'll usually have him safely crated or protected by a seat belt during transport, try to get someone else to drive during this first trip home while you cuddle up in the back seat with your precious new companion. Because he is liable to be nervous or even frightened, this is the time to hold him close and speak lovingly to him. In no time at all, he'll probably be asleep!

Establishing Routines

Both puppies and older adopted dogs really rely on regular routines and structure to build their confidence and give them a sense of security. A dog who never knows when he's going to be fed next will be constantly whining for dinner. A dog who never knows when walk time is will demand to go out all the time. A dog who is uncertain when he gets to play with you will be forever begging you to play a game. This doesn't mean that you can't ever forget the routine or give him extra attention; it does mean, though, that he should expect certain things at certain times. Although it may seem like a chore to develop a fixed routine for your puppy, in the long run it will make life a lot easier for both of you.

Enforcing rules consistently from the time your German Shepherd Dog is a puppy will make it easier for him to learn. Saying no is sometimes harder on the owner than it is on the dog!

Elementary Training

Your new dog, whether puppy or adult, should learn the following things about your house within the first few days:

- Where his food and water dishes are
- When he gets fed
- Where his crate or bed is located
- When he gets to go out
- When people get up and go to bed
- Where his toys are

Knowing these things will help make him comfortable and confident. Dogs whose schedules are switched, food bowls moved around, and who are subjected to varying times for walks have more trouble housetraining and just figuring out their place in the world.

In most cases, your German Shepherd Dog will figure things out on his own, but if he's having trouble, you may have to show him. Soon, he'll figure out the word "no." He'll hear it often enough. But never let "no!" be the end of your training. If your GSD is doing something you don't want, such as teething on your hand or chewing your

The Dog Act

In the United Kingdom, the 1906 (that's right—1906) Dog Act requires that all dogs whilst on the "public highways" must wear a collar with their owners' name and address inscribed or attached to it.

shoes, offer him a replacement item. Puppies have to do something; they are not stuffed animals.

Unfortunately, most of the things they can think of to do are dangerous or damaging. You are the human, and you are supposed to be the smart one. Thus, you need to figure out something your dog can do that is not damaging or dangerous. This almost inevitably requires you to interact with him!

Most important is that your puppy learns that you are a trusted, loving, gentle leader. If you can get that across, everything else is a piece of cake.

SUPPLIES

Like new babies, new dogs need a plethora of supplies. The following items will help your German Shepherd Dog settle into his new home.

Crate

A crate, one made of wire or heavy-duty molded plastic, will make housetraining your GSD much easier. (See Chapter 6 for more information on housetraining your GSD.) It will also function as a safe "den" for the puppy.

Dogs are social animals who want to be with their people. For this reason, it is usually best to place the crate near where family members spend most of their time. Wire is more portable and ventilates better than plastic or plexiglas. Plastic crates, however,

like the ones Nylabone makes, are safer, often easier to transport, more comforting to the pet, and usually less expensive. You may wish to get one of each!

Dogs try not to eliminate in their bedding area, so don't make it too large. You can buy dividers for puppies to ease housetraining.

Never crate a puppy for more than two or three hours except at night when he should be sleeping. German Shepherd Dogs need plenty of opportunities to exercise their minds and bodies. Overuse of the crate can lead to terrible behavior problems for bored and lonely dogs.

Food and Water Bowls

Glass and ceramic bowls are breakable, and puppies love to chew plastic. (Some dogs also have allergic reactions to plastic.) Stainless steel is a better choice. Get a 2-quart stainless bowl for food and a 2-quart or larger stainless pail for water.

Food Containers and Scoops

If you choose not to feed directly out the bag, buy a made-to-order pet food container. Don't use a trash can, even a new one, which can exude odors and chemicals that make the food smell and taste bad. A durable scooper will make serving the food easier, too.

Doggie Door

If you have a securely fenced yard or garden, doggie doors make housetraining easier. You can buy adjustable ones that will keep your puppy safe inside if you don't want him outside. The large size is fine for the GSD.

Pooper-Scooper

Several varieties of pooper-scoopers are available. The advantage of a pooper-scooper is that it saves your back and keeps your nose distant from the object you are picking up. On the other hand, a pooper-scooper is never around at the right time, and it can be a little awkward to carry. You can purchase bags designed for scooping, but a plain plastic grocery bag works just as well and is much cheaper.

Multiple Dogs

If you already own a dog, let the older dog know that company is on the way. You can help prepare your older dog for the big event by setting up crates in the house in advance, and if possible, bringing home a towel or T-shirt imbued with the new dog's scent.

Introduce the pets to each other slowly. Many a young pup has been seriously injured by a grouchy older dog. Do not leave them unsupervised. While many people can raise two German Shepherd Dogs, adding a third dog to the group becomes exponentially more difficult. I don't recommend adding a third dog unless you are extremely knowledgeable about the breed.

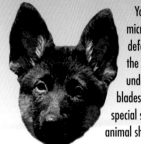

Microchipping Your German Shepherd Dog

You should get your dog microchipped as a second line of defense. The microchip is a pellet the size of a rice grain. It is slipped under the skin between the shoulder blades. The chip can be "read" by special scanners at humane societies, animal shelters, and many vet clinics.

Bedding

As a crate liner, choose bedding made from tough but soft acrylic fleece. Any liquid can pass through this substance, leaving the pup warm and dry. This bedding is cut from the roll to any length you need. It can also be machine washed.

Collar

Your dog should wear a buckle collar and ID tag at all times. Collars are lifesavers—literally. In case of emergency, your German Shepherd Dog can be held and safely restrained by his collar. Most importantly, a collar carries that indispensable ID tag. Although I also encourage you to get your dog microchipped, a lost dog with visible identification is most likely to be returned to his owner.

Adjust your German Shepherd Dog's collar so that you can insert four fingers under it, and if you have a puppy, check it frequently to make sure it's big enough. However, don't make it so loose your dog could wriggle out of it on a walk.

Choke Collars

The biggest debate surrounds the use of choke (slip) collars. Unfortunately, the incorrect use of these devices can result in a neck injury, especially for a puppy. Some trainers object to the "punishment" aspect of choke collars, maintaining that owners will achieve better, longer-lasting results using positive reinforcement techniques and plain old buckle collars. In my opinion, the less force (or correction) you need to train your dog, the easier the training, and the closer the bond between you and your dog will be. I would begin training with a flat buckle collar.

Head Halters

The head halter is an alternative to a conventional collar. It is humane and safe and works by controlling the head so that the body will follow. People have been leading horses around with halters for centuries; a dog-sized version isn't too different. Proper fitting is really essential, though. One drawback to the halter is that it can only be worn when there is human supervision; left alone, your puppy can get it caught in something as he explores his surroundings. In addition, many dogs may fight it, possibly because they can't put their heads down and sniff around with the ease to which they are accustomed. While most dogs eventually become acclimated to the collar, others may not adapt as quickly. The fact is that a lot of dogs really dislike these, no matter how humane they are.

Harnesses

Some people prefer harnesses, especially for puppies. Harnesses are also good for dogs with spinal problems or for sensitive dogs who don't like collars and head halters. They are very safe but provide less control than other methods. However, there are some exceptions. One new harness recently developed has a loop low on the front at the bottom of the chest instead of along the back, which causes resistance to pulling and makes walking a breeze.

Leash or Lead

You should also have a regular 4- to 6-foot leash (lead) made of leather, waxed cotton, or nylon. Chain leashes are noisy, heavy, and unnecessary. They give no warning when they are about to break, and they can develop sharp edges. Good leather leads are durable and comfortable, especially

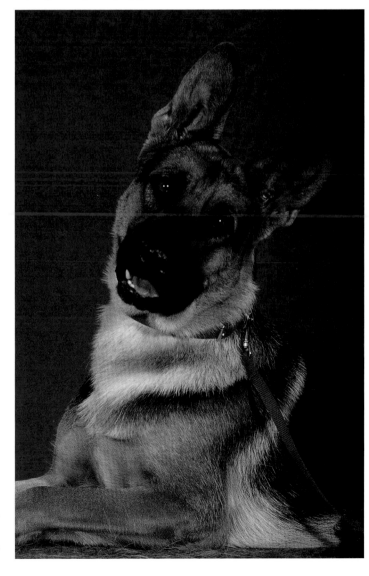

You will need a collar and leash to begin training your German Shepherd Dog.

as they age. Beware of cheap leather leashes, however, which can be rough on your hands. The downside of leather leashes is that they are slow to dry out once they get wet. They are also attractive to dogs' taste buds. Never let your German Shepherd Dog take the leash in his mouth. Once he gets a taste for it, you're doomed. (Some owners spray their leather leashes with a bitter apple spray or a similar aversive product to discourage chewing.)

Teach your puppy to accept the lead by leaving a short one on him for a while. Supervise him the entire time so that he doesn't catch the lead on anything or chew it to pieces. He will probably fuss with it a bit at first, but he'll soon get used to it. When you do pick up the end, follow him for a while. When you take the lead yourself, call the puppy to you gently; when he toddles up to you, give him a treat and praise him. Very soon he will be happily following you everywhere. At this stage, try not to struggle with your puppy. If he resists, don't tug the other way, but don't give in either. Lure him to you with a biscuit. He'll soon catch on that it's fun to do what he's asked. Keep puppy lessons short—five minutes a couple of times a day is enough.

Toys that do not have small parts, such as latex toys and rubber bones, are safest for your puppy.

Toys

Choose toys that do not have small, easily removable parts, and throw them away as soon as they start to fall apart. Toys (especially balls) that are too small can be swallowed easily. Nylabones, latex squeaky toys, rubber bones and balls, and faux lamb's wool plush toys are all excellent choices. However, not all puppies are equal, and not all should have the same toys. Destructive chewers should be given only durable hard rubber or nylon toys. Aggressive but not

destructive chewers are safe with canvas, fleece, or plush toys. Don't buy too many in the beginning, though, as your dog may become overwhelmed or bored—rotate them and keep enough around to prevent your pup from chewing on the forbidden furniture.

Prevent your German Shepherd Dog from getting into trouble indoors by supervising him closely and limiting him to dog-proofed rooms.

You may want to avoid stick-type rawhide chews, as they can become stuck in your dog's throat. In addition, refrain from giving your German Shepherd Dog toys that require batteries, because he could swallow them.

Grooming Supplies

Grooming supplies for your German Shepherd Dog include brushes and combs, shampoo/conditioner, canine toothpaste and toothbrush, nail clippers, and ear cleaner. Useful brushes include a rubber curry brush and a slicker brush. For the shedding season, a shedding blade is also helpful. (Learn about grooming in Chapter 5.)

Baby Gate

Baby or specially designed dog gates are essential for keeping the dog out of any room you don't want him in. Don't get a

A secure fence is essential for keeping your German Shepherd Dog safely confined while outdoors.

wooden gate, though, as your German Shepherd Dog may be inclined to chew right through it.

Because you will need to block off certain rooms and the stairway, you should choose a baby gate that's approved by consumer organizations. You can even purchase some made especially for dogs!

Exercise Pen

This portable puppy playpen is a compromise between the isolation of the crate and the free range of the kitchen or living room. During times when you want your puppy near you but not underfoot, the so-called x-pen ("x" is for "exercise") is a great way to oversee his activities. While you are cooking dinner or cleaning the refrigerator, your puppy can watch you. Even more importantly, you can keep an eye on him. Watch for those telltale squirming signs, and you can use the x-pen as a housetraining tool as well as a containment device.

Anti-Chew Spray

Puppies chew. Chewing is not only important for properly setting their teeth, but it's also the way in which they explore the world. Your job is to direct and supervise the chewing to appropriate objects. An anti-chew spray will help in this regard by giving a tempting but inappropriate object an awful taste, thus discouraging the dog from chomping down on it.

Car Seat Belts or Other Restraint

If you plan to travel with your dog, don't allow him to run loose in the car. A safety restraint will keep you and your German Shepherd Dog much safer.

PUPPY-PROOFING YOUR HOME

The German Shepherd Dog is a slow-maturing breed with a protracted puppyhood, so you will have to be especially vigilant and supervise him as closely as possible. Your puppy will run into things, chew things, knock things over with his tail, and generally create a happy rumpus wherever he goes.

Preparing for disasters is the only way to avoid them. This is why it's important to decide before you bring your puppy home which areas will be his to explore (with your supervision) and which will be off-limits. Protect the off-limits areas with baby gates.

Indoors

Your house is a veritable garden of temptation for a curious puppy: smelly sneakers, interesting electrical cords, window cords and drapes, medicines, you name it. A good way to puppy-proof your home is to look at it from a dog's eye view. Lock away valuable keepsakes and dangerous cleaners. Keep doors shut to areas you want to remain off-limits, especially closet and cabinets. Hide electric cords, or tape them to the wall and spray them with an anti-chew spray. Keep kitchen supplies like aluminum and plastic food wrap away from your puppy, as they can be very dangerous to your dog. (These items are very tempting to dogs because they smell like food.) If ingested, aluminum foil can cut a dog's intestines, causing internal bleeding. Plastic food wrap can cause choking or intestinal obstruction. In addition, all trash cans should be made inaccessible. Highly scented items (flowers, trash, candles) are irresistible. Older dogs are not apt to chew them, but young ones will. Finally, potentially toxic foods, like chocolate, should be kept away from your dog. Chocolate contains a toxic substance called theobromine that can poison your dog, causing symptoms like vomiting, diarrhea, tremors, hyperactivity, and seizures. Dark and unsweetened baking chocolates are especially

The Dangers of Xylitol

According to the Animal Poison Control Center, since July 2003, more than 45 animals have been reported sick after devouring gum or candy containing xylitol, a sugar-alcohol sweetener found in some chewing gum and candy. Dogs who eat significant amounts can develop a sudden drop in blood sugar, which can cause weakness, lethargy, loss of coordination, collapse, and seizures. Signs can begin in as little as 30 minutes after ingestion and last for hours. If your dog is a victim, he needs to be hospitalized and given intravenous fluids with dextrose supplementation.

dangerous. Tobacco is another common poison that can be lethal to pets. For most poisonings, there isn't much you can do at home. Call your veterinarian or veterinary emergency facility if you suspect your pet has been poisoned.

The best way to prevent disaster is to supervise your puppy and not allow him to have the run of the house. That is an invitation to disaster!

Outdoors

A Doggy "Don't"

Never tie your dog outside unsupervised. It's dangerous and cruel. I once knew a lovely dog who was stung almost to death when tied outside with no supervision. He uncovered a hornet's nest and was unable to escape.

Your yard or garden may be your puppy's playpen, but it can be dangerous, too. (It's even more dangerous outside of it, so make sure you keep the fence in good repair.) First, never allow your pup in the garage without close supervision. Ethylene-glycol

Children and German Shepherd Dogs need to be socialized toward one another.

Children and German Shepherd Dogs

German Shepherd Dogs are loyal family members and reliable protectors of children. However, both children and dogs need to be properly socialized toward one another in order to make the relationship work. Remember, it's up to parents to teach children how to safely and properly interact with puppies. Children are not born with this knowledge. Unfortunately, many parents simply expect that a puppy and their kids should be able to get along and tolerate one another. This does not happen automatically.

Teaching proper manners for both dogs and children should begin as early as possible before the puppy even arrives. You can play the "dog" and teach the child the correct way to approach and pet you. Dogs are living, animate creatures, not toys. Just as you would teach a puppy not to nip or jump, children need to learn not to squeeze, pinch, hit, or kick. They should also learn never to disturb the dog when he is eating, chewing a rawhide, or sleeping. Perhaps most importantly, no dog should be left alone with a young child for any reason.

Children can learn proper behavior around a dog very early, even by the age of two or three. If you cannot trust your child not to poke or irritate a dog, though, don't get one until the child is older or you have him or her under better control. Toddlers and GSD puppies should be together only under close adult supervision.

Older children can accept some responsibility for taking care of the family pet, but as the adult in the family, you are the one ultimately responsible for the dog's well-being. Begin by allowing the child to help you walk, feed, bathe, train, and take your GSD to the vet for a checkup.

While walking, teach your child how to hold the dog's lead. Explain that he must make sure the dog stays off other people's property and out of the street. You can give your older child simple jobs such as keeping the water bowl full or at least telling you when it is empty. By ten years of age, your child should be able to feed the dog as well as do cleanup duty in the yard.

antifreeze, fertilizers, pesticides, paint, and nails are lurking there just waiting to harm your dog. If ingested, sweet-tasting antifreeze is often fatal, even in tiny amounts. Poisoning from antifreeze is a serious medical emergency that must be treated by a veterinarian immediately.

If you use an insecticide or other chemicals on your lawn, follow label instructions to the letter. Allow the product to dry before permitting pets and people into the yard. Most products are safe once they are dry and bound to the grass.

To keep your dog safer from ticks, keep grass mowed and leaf litter picked up. Most environments are particularly attractive to fleas and ticks. To reduce the number of disease-carrying mosquitoes, eliminate areas of standing water where they breed; that includes cans, old tires, and clogged drain gutters. Change the water in outdoor pet bowls every day and twice weekly for wading pools and bird baths. If you have an ornamental pond, stock it with goldfish, who feed on mosquitoes and mosquito larva.

Many common flowers, bulbs, and bushes (like boxwood) are

poisonous to dogs. This is why you should never let the puppy explore on his own until you have inspected the yard first. Choose an area outside that will serve as your puppy's potty area. This is more convenient for both of you. It makes it easier for him to identify the acceptable elimination area and also lessens the possibility of you stepping in something untoward.

Ice-melting chemicals and salt placed across sidewalks, walkways, and roads can cause severe burning to your dog's footpads. Whenever possible, avoid walking your dog through these substances, and wash off his footpads when you return home from your winter walks. There are also products available that can be applied to your dog's footpads prior to going outside that may help reduce the pain that is often caused by road salt and chemicals.

HOW TO KEEP YOUR GERMAN SHEPHERD DOG HAPPY

The GSD needs lots of exercise to keep him from becoming depressed or destructive.

If you were a dog, how would you rate yourself as an owner? How good are you at providing for his needs? Like people, dogs need both routine and adventure. They also need a secure social network and plenty of love. It's not enough to say you love your

dog, though—you have to show him. The following are some ways that you can show your German Shepherd Dog just how much you love him.

- Let him get enough sleep. Dogs need 10 to 12 hours of sleep a day and can become grouchy if they don't get it.
- Give him positive and consistent experiences. Let him meet other dogs and people, and let him look forward to each new day with you.
- Give him a reliable but not boring schedule. Regular feedings and exercise reduce stress. That doesn't mean you can't surprise him with an extra walk, ride, or activity once in a while, though!
- Let him learn. German Shepherd Dogs are highly intelligent and enjoy learning new things. The average GSD can learn a new word every month. Make it fun for him.
- Keep him healthy. A sick pet is a sad pet. Regular checkups and appropriate diet and exercise are the keys to a healthy German Shepherd Dog.
- Feed him well. A highly nutritious and interesting diet makes dogs happy, as food is one of their greatest joys in life.
- Give him sufficient exercise. The GSD craves exercise, and if he doesn't get it, he will become dull, antisocial, depressed, or destructive. These dogs were not meant to be shut up in an apartment eight or ten hours every day while you go off to work. They expect to be tending sheep, or at the very least leading the blind, looking for lost kids, or chasing down bad guys. If none of these activities are available to the two of you, then you'll need to substitute with obedience, agility, tracking, flyball, hiking, skijoring, or any one of numerous other dog activities. You may have to reorient your social life, but at least your dog will be happy. Your German Shepherd Dog needs at least 30 minutes of vigorous exercise every day.

Pet Travel Scheme (PETS)

PETS is a system that permits companion animals from certain countries to travel to the UK without undergoing a period of quarantine. This scheme also applies to people in the UK who want to travel with their pets to other European Union countries. For more information, visit the Department for Environment Food and Rural Affairs' website at www.defra.gov.uk.

TRAVEL

Traveling is more fun with a German Shepherd Dog at your side. After all, these dogs were born to be our companions!

If You Go Away Without Him

Alas, you can't always take your dog with you. However, whether you're near or far, your precious GSD trusts you to do the

When traveling by car, restrain your dog with a seat belt to prevent him from injuring himself or the driver.

best you can for him in the way of comfort and entertainment while you're gone.

House Sitters

You may be lucky enough to have a trusted friend or family member drop by regularly to take care of your German Shepherd Dog. The ideal person would not only feed, walk, and clean up after him, but also play with him, cuddle him, and perhaps clean the oven. But maybe that's asking too much. If you can't get somebody to take on the task for free or next to nothing, you might consider engaging the services of a professional house sitter.

Boarding Kennels

Another option is the boarding kennel, but they fill up fast, so you'll have to plan ahead. When you find a potential kennel, call and ask if you can visit. Take your dog along. Not only will you be able to gauge the staff's response to him, but when he returns for

Finding the Lost GSD

While you certainly don't intend to lose your dog, it can happen. To help retrieve your GSD as quickly as possible, keep a recent photo of your dog on file, either as a print or digital image. It's also smart to prepare a few dozen flyers before the dog actually becomes lost, so all you have to do is post them around the neighborhood and at the local veterinarians' offices. Take one to the shelter, too. Don't simply call them and ask if your dog is there. Bring them a flyer and look for yourself.

If you lose your dog, don't wait around. Take immediate action. The longer your dog is gone, the less chance you have of getting him back. Consider enlisting the help of the neighborhood kids for a reward. However, if your dog is reserved around children or doesn't like them, you will have to look all by yourself. GSDs are not strayers or wanderers, so if your dog goes missing, chances are that he has been stolen or injured. This is why checking vet clinics is critical, as is keeping him safe behind tall, locked gates.

his stay, it won't be a completely new experience. Good boarding kennels should feature the following:

- The staff should be polite, friendly, and knowledgeable about dogs.
- The facility should be clean and well ventilated, with large kennels. Beware of overcrowding. Good kennels not only look clean but smell that way, too. Good kennels have heating and air-conditioning.
- The other dogs should be in good condition and look happy.
- The best kennels have convenient hours, are willing to feed your dog his own food (you have to bring it), and will allow you, bring your dog's blanket and toys.

Pet Sitters

More than 10 million homes will be visited by a pet sitter this year. For dog owners, pet sitting provides a great alternative to kennels or the maybe not-so-reliable neighbor. A pet sitter will visit your home every day to feed, walk, medicate, and play with your pet. Dogs love the comfort of staying home (even if you're not there), and you will have the comfort of knowing that someone is checking up on the homestead. Pet sitters belonging to Pet Sitters International or a similar organization are bonded, have liability insurance, and are professionally accredited.

FEEDING

Your German Shepherd Dog

Probably no other topic stirs the passions of dedicated dog owners as deeply as nutrition does. Grocery aisles, pet supply stores, and Internet retailers hawk their own special brands. Websites, magazines, and veterinary journals proclaim the values (or dangers) of certain supplements, vitamins, or methods of preparing homecooked food. There are more brands of dog food available than almost any other consumable, with the possible exception of kids' cereal.

Adventurous dining is the hallmark of this adaptable species. Dogs have evolved to survive on garbage. Whether the garbage comes from the trash can or the dog food can makes little difference (except that food from the former may taste better). Dogs take whatever they can find, and they eat it. They are the ultimate survivors. However, good nutrition not only helps your dog feel his best and perform at his optimum level, it makes him look great, too!

DIET BASICS: NUTRIENTS

Your dog's health depends upon whether or not he receives the right amounts and proportions of the correct nutrients. A nutrient is a dietary component that has a particular function. Nutrients that the body can manufacture on its own from other nutrients are called "nonessential." Those nutrients that the body needs to import in their final form are called "essential." The nutrients your dog needs work synergistically. For example, a specific metabolic reaction may take ten steps, each requiring a different nutrient. If even one of these nutrients is missing or deficient, it's as if all ten were missing. Factors influencing how much of a particular nutrient a dog needs include genetic makeup, environmental toxins, age, stress, illness, injury, diet, exercise, and medications.

There are six classes of nutrients: water, proteins, fat, carbohydrates, minerals, and vitamins.

Water

Water, the basis of good nutrition, is the most important substance of all. Your dog needs more water than anything else in his diet, and he will die sooner without water than without food. If a dog becomes more than 12 percent dehydrated, he will die. Water performs the following functions:

- Carries other nutrients
- Flushes waste
- Aids certain chemical reactions
- Helps regulate body temperature
- Provides shape and resilience to the body

About 70 percent of your dog's lean body mass is water. Water is stored in the body in four different "compartments." About 64 percent resides within the cells; 22 percent lies in the intercellular spaces; 7 percent is in the blood plasma; and the remaining 7 percent is present as transcellular fluid in the eyes, cerebral spinal fluid, joint (synovial) fluid, and digestive secretions.

Provide fresh water at all times, even in the winter when you might get tricked into thinking dogs don't need as much. Remember that winter homes are dryer, which increases a dog's water requirement. Wash the water bowl regularly.

Proteins

Proteins are long, complex molecules comprised of amino acids strung together like beads on a chain, and they compose about 50 percent of every cell. Proteins are also critical in building enzymes, hormones, hemoglobin, and antibodies. All animals need protein for maintenance, and young animals need it for growth. If a puppy doesn't get enough protein, his tissues and organs won't develop properly. A low-quality protein is one that is less digestible or that lacks essential amino acids. Dogs on a poor or low-protein diet suffer muscle degeneration, skeletal anomalies, and develop a poor coat.

Protein quality is even more important than the quantity of protein your German Shepherd Dog receives. Protein quality is partly determined by its amino acid content. In general, dogs need about 3 grams of high-quality protein per kilogram of body weight

Nutritional Levels

In 1985, the National Research Council (NRC) established the basic nutrient needs of dogs, but it left wide and sometimes critical margins. There is a big difference between the minimum a dog needs to survive (the minimum daily requirement, or MDR) and recommended daily allowances (RDA). (There is also a maximum level—the amount over which a substance may be toxic.) Most good commercial foods provide the RDA.

daily. The higher the quality of protein, the less a dog needs. A diet of 10 percent high-quality protein (meat and eggs) is equal to a diet containing 22 percent protein derived from cereal. Puppies on a low-protein diet will not grow well, and dogs of all ages will be more susceptible to disease. Too much protein in the diet is only harmful if the dog has bad kidneys. (Unused protein is normally excreted with the help of the kidneys.)

For most dogs, meat is the prime provider of protein and its constituent amino acids. Puppies and older dogs require more protein, while dogs in their prime need less. Theories vary about how much meat should be in a dog's diet; estimates range from as high as 75 percent to as low as 25 percent. A lower number is fine if supplemented with eggs and dairy.

Fats

Dogs can use both plant and animal fats (lipids) with equal ease. However, oils derived from plants provide large amounts of essential fatty acids (EFAs). These acids are essential for many biological functions.

Water is the basis of good nutrition, and your German Shepherd Dog needs more water in his diet than anything else.

Lipids have the following functions:
- Supply energy
- Make up the main part of membranes surrounding cells
- Carry the fat-soluble vitamins A, D, E, and K and aid in their absorption in the body
- Provide essential fatty acids
- Help make calcium more available to the body

Dogs and people not only use fat, but they store it as well. Dogs store fat under their skin, around their vital organs, and in the membranes surrounding the intestines. Fat storage serves not only as an energy reserve but as an insulator against both cold and injury. Of course, there's such a thing as too much fat, a condition known as obesity. It occurs when an animal (or

Puppies need protein in their diets to help them grow and develop properly.

person) takes in more calories through food than is expended through exercise.

Carbohydrates

There is no minimum dietary level for carbohydrates in the canine diet. However, when present, they perform the following functions (which can also be performed by proteins and fats):

- Provide energy
- Supply a heat source for the body when metabolized for energy
- Serve as building blocks for other biological components, such as glycoproteins, vitamin C, nonessential amino acids, glycolipids, and lactose
- Can be stored as glycogen or converted to fat
- Help regulate protein and fat metabolism

Nearly all commercial dry dog foods are based on carbohydrates in the form of grain and cereal products. As long as growing and adult dogs get enough fat and protein in their diets, dogs don't require carbohydrates, although they can utilize them well.

Nutritional factors that play an important role in immune function include zinc, selenium, vitamin E, vitamin B6 (pyridoxine), and linoleic acid. Deficiencies of these compounds impair both circulation and cell-mediated immunity.

Fiber

One type of carbohydrate is fiber. Fiber performs a balancing act, and it is said to normalize the digestive process of dogs with constipation and dogs with diarrhea. First, it speeds the passage of food through the stomach, often before it is fully broken down. It then slows the passage down through the lower part of the small intestine and colon. In dogs with diarrhea, fiber serves as a natural laxative and stool softener. (By distending the large intestine, it stimulates defecation.) On the other hand, fiber helps manage diarrhea by regulating the system. Thus, dogs with all kinds of bowel problems are often put on a high-fiber diet.

Too much fiber can be bad, particularly if the fiber is expandable, like beet pulp, cellulose, or tomato pomace. This is because if the food is not completely broken down as it passes through the small intestine, the body may not recognize it as food and may attack the "foreign bodies," causing allergic and autoimmune reactions.

Minerals

Dietary minerals are classed into three groups: macrominerals (sulfur, calcium, phosphorus, magnesium, and the electrolytes sodium, potassium, and chloride), which are consumed in gram amounts per day; trace minerals (iron, zinc, copper, iodine, and selenium), which are needed in milligram or microgram amounts per day (these "microminerals" can be toxic if taken in high doses); and ultratrace minerals (like beryllium), which have been shown to be necessary in laboratory animals but not in dogs.

Minerals participate in nearly every function of the body. They build teeth and bone, serve as enzyme cofactors, and are a vital part of the blood and other body fluids. Minerals also play a role in muscle contraction, the transmission of nerve impulses, and in cell membrane permeability. One of the unusual things about minerals is the way in which they interact. The action of one often enhances, is necessary for, or impedes the action of another. These interactions can occur during digestion, at the tissue storage site, during transport out of the digestive system, or even within the pathways of excretion.

Not every mineral in the world has importance in the diet. Some, like cadmium, lead, and mercury, are harmful in any amounts, and gold and silver, while not harmful, don't do your

Carb Considerations

Some dogs cannot digest carbohydrates well. This can be due to a deficiency of digestive enzymes, which means that adding digestive enzymes to the diet may help. Sometimes it's because the energy-dependent transport system that helps absorb glucose from the intestine isn't all it could be. Sometimes an infection or disease is the cause. Dogs with this problem may have diarrhea, gas, and abdominal distention. For these dogs, I recommend that people select food with a fairly low carb count.

Your German Shepherd Dog stores fat as an energy reserve and as an insulator against the cold.

dog any good either. (This is a good thing, because gold supplements would cost a lot more than calcium supplements!)

It is very tricky to supplement minerals, because supplementation of any one mineral can create imbalances or interfere with another. While supplementation is sometimes needed to correct an imbalance, this is something that should be addressed in consultation with your veterinarian.

Vitamins

Vitamins are plant- and animal-derived substances necessary for your dog's health. Your dog needs only an infinitesimal amount of vitamins in his diet, but that tiny amount is absolutely essential. To qualify as a bona fide vitamin, a substance must be:

- An organic compound different from proteins, fats, or carbohydrates
- A component of the diet
- Critical for normal body functioning and whose absence produces a deficiency syndrome
- Not synthesized in quantities sufficient to support normal physiologic function

Vitamins are divided into two types: fat soluble (A, D, E, and K) and water soluble (C and the eight B vitamins). Fat-soluble vitamins need dietary fat in order to be absorbed from the gut and taken up into the body, while water-soluble vitamins need only water. Fat-soluble vitamins are handled by the body in the same way as dietary fat—the metabolites of these vitamins are excreted

in the feces. Excess fat-soluble vitamins are stored in the liver and can be toxic if too much is eaten. Water-soluble vitamins (except for B₁₂) are not stored in the body and need to be replaced regularly. Most water-soluble vitamins are absorbed in the small intestine and excreted in the urine.

Minerals participate in nearly every function of the body, including muscle contraction.

Vitamins play one or more of these roles in the body:
- Act as potentiators or cofactors in enzymatic reactions
- Help synthesize DNA

Supplements

Many people believe that if a healthy dog is getting good food, supplements are not needed. This is usually true. The only problem is that even canine nutritionists are not completely sure what composes a good food. In addition, not all dogs are completely healthy, in which case it may make sense to add a little something extra to the diet.

Do not supplement minerals like calcium or phosphorous except at the direction of your veterinarian. Supplementing the carefully balanced minerals in your dog's food can lead to trouble. The same is true of certain fat-soluble vitamins like A and D; these vitamins are stored in the liver and can be toxic in large doses. (Vitamin E, another fat-soluble vitamin, does not appear to have toxic effects and may be supplemented if desired.)

Before you purchase a supplement, check out the source. Use a product that was designed for animals, even if it uses human-grade ingredients, as it should. The best supplements carry the Good Manufacturing Practices Certificate (GMP) and the ConsumerLab (CL) seal of approval. In addition, if the product has been produced according to the United States Pharmacopoeia (USP) guidelines, the label will say so. You should also look for organically grown herbs where possible.

- Scavenge free radicals
- Release energy from nutrients
- Maintain cell membrane integrity
- Help bone development
- Help maintain calcium homeostasis
- Aid normal eye function
- Help nerve impulse transduction
- Help blood clot

FEEDING METHODS

You have three basic choices when it comes to serving grub: free feeding, timed feeding, and food-restricted meal feeding. For the German Shepherd Dog, food-restricted meal feeding is the best.

Vitamins play an important role in your German Shepherd Dog's diet.

The amount you feed your dog should depend on his activity level and particular metabolism. I suggest that you follow the manufacturer's feeding labels; 1 cup of one food is not the same calorie-wise as that of another. Observe how your dog does when following the manufacturer's recommendations, and add or decrease the amount of food as needed.

Free Feeding

When free feeding, you simply put down all the food your dog could reasonably be expected to eat during the day and forget about it. Obviously, this is the easiest method for you, but it's not usually a good idea, especially if you have multiple dogs. The dominant dog may get all the food and leave the more submissive dogs without anything to eat. In addition, a free-fed dog in a multiple-dog household who goes off his feed may not be noticed for several days.

Free feeding also encourages a dog to eat throughout the day. Not only is this unnatural, it also causes

Choosing a food-restricted meal feeding plan is usually the best option for most dog owners.

your dog to be more lethargic and get less exercise because he's burning up calories digesting his food. Consequently, you can end up with an overweight dog.

Timed Feeding

With timed feeding, you give your dog a certain period of time to eat, usually between 10 and 15 minutes, then take the food away. Most dogs eat their entire dinner in a minute or so anyway, so this method is primarily used by people who are dealing with a picky eater. Timed feeding may encourage a picky eater to eat better, but the disadvantage is that you have to stand around timing your dog.

Food-Restricted Meal Feeding

The best choice for most owners is the food-restricted meal feeding. Simply serve the dog his dinner and walk away. Pick up the empty bowl later. This method gives you control over the dog's intake and doesn't put an unnatural pressure on him to "eat up" or else not have anything to eat at all.

Most experts believe feeding two smaller meals a day is better than one large one. There is some evidence that dogs fed only one large meal a day produce more stomach acid; this can lead to irritation of the esophagus. On the other hand, wild dogs are lucky to eat even once a day. But who knows what their esophagi look like?

Why Do Dogs Eat Grass?

Why do dogs eat grass, anyway? No one knows for sure, although theories abound. Some have claimed that dogs eat grass because they feel unwell and know it will make them vomit. Others claim that dogs simply like the way grass tastes!

DOG FOOD LABELS

In the United States, 95 percent of dogs receive nearly all of their nutrition from commercial pet food, which means that although owners have literally hundreds of commercial brands to choose from, they need to educate themselves about what they're buying. Although dog food labels are not written in classical Greek, they might as well be as far as the average dog owner is concerned. One reason for this is that the pet food label is actually a legal document. Legal documents are incomprehensible by their very nature. If nothing else, remember this: A dog food label can hide a lot more than it is required—or even permitted—to reveal. "Buyer beware" is definitely the rule to follow.

The FDA's Center for Veterinary Medicine requires manufacturers merely to provide the following information on the dog food label. (None of this means the product is any good. It just means that it's properly labeled.)

1. Accurately identify the product. This means that the product must be labeled "cat food," "hamster food," or "dog food." It must also include the brand name of the product. The brand name and product name are both subject to regulation by the Association of American Feed Control Officials (AAFCO).
2. Provide the net quantity of the food by weight (not volume).
3. Give the manufacturer's name and address.
4. Correctly list ingredients. Manufacturers are not required by the feds to list the ingredients in any particular order, although it's their general practice to list the ingredients in order of the amount present in the food. However, many states require that the ingredients be listed in a particular order.

In addition, all pet foods must be registered with state feed control officials, who insist that the ingredients be what they call GRAS (generally regarded as safe). However, pet food companies are not required to state where or when a food was manufactured, information that could help consumers.

Dog food labels are divided into two parts, or panels. One part is the principal display panel, and the second is the ingredient list or information panel. The principal display panel is the bait, but the information panel gives you the real goods. The information panel must include the following: ingredient list, guaranteed analysis, nutritional adequacy statement, feeding guidelines, and manufacturer. It may also include calorie information, a freshness date, batch identification, and universal product code. Because companies do not have to say what percentage of their product is meat, they don't. They only have to say how much protein is in the food. And since a lot of the protein is low-quality plant protein, it's understandable (although not forgivable) that the manufacturers don't reveal how much real meat is in the food.

TYPES OF FOOD

Dogs are designed behaviorally to enjoy a wide variety of foods, just as humans are. This sensible practice has helped them survive through hard times over the millennia. And like humans, although they can thrive on one balanced food year in and year out, they would prefer a change.

You'll know your GSD is getting the nutrients he needs if his energy is up, his eyes are shiny, and his coat is lustrous.

Feeding your dog a variety of foods increases the chance that he is getting complete nutrition. Variety also gives the dog's digestive system a workout and makes his eating experience more pleasant, natural, and interesting. Like healthy people, healthy dogs thrive on variety, although a few exhibit signs like vomiting, diarrhea, belching, or flatulence. (This might mean that your dog's digestive system isn't all that it should be.) If you wish to be more cautious, you can change your German Shepherd Dog's food over a three to seven day period. You may take even longer if the diet change is really significant or if your dog has reacted poorly to food changes in the past. Change your dog's diet by gradually mixing in the new food with the old until the change is complete.

A highly variable diet is so palatable to dogs that you may notice your dog gaining weight, simply because he is for the first time really enjoying his food. If that's the case, cut back on the amount he is eating while making sure he is getting a full array of nutrients.

Commercial Foods

Dog food should taste good, at least to the dogs. If you have to lure, beg, bribe, or threaten an otherwise healthy dog to eat commercial food,

Meat Meal

It is best not to buy products with the generic term "meat meal" on a label, because you have no idea what the source of the meat is.

it probably isn't very tasty, and you're creating unneeded stress for both of you. Some say, "Well, just keep offering him the food long enough, and don't give him anything else—he'll eat it eventually." Your dog probably would, rather than starve to death, but that doesn't mean he'll find mealtime enjoyable. Others claim that offering a less palatable food will lead your pet to consume less food. This seems ridiculous to me. Eating is one of life's great joys. Keep your dog trim by feeding him just the right amount of nutritious, tasty food that he requires. If he's getting fat, feed him less and exercise him more. The only reason I can think of for serving less palatable foods would be to slow down a greedy dog's eating rate.

Most pet food manufacturers perform palatability studies comparing the target brand of food with other kinds. However, be aware that some dog foods are made artificially palatable by the inclusion of ingredients that not only provide no benefit but may actually be harmful to your pet. Artificial flavor enhancers include sugars, digests, processed meat flavors, yeast products, garlic, cheese, and bacon flavors, as well as "masking" flavors designed to hide the odor of the original food.

Rather than give a list of poor-quality dog foods, here are some ingredients you may want to avoid in a variety of foods:

- **Artificial preservatives.** Artificial preservatives include things like propyl gallate, BHA, BHT, and ethoxyquin. Not only do some dogs react adversely to these preservatives, but there are serious questions about their safety. Choose foods that use natural preservatives like vitamins C and E (tocopherols) to avoid potential problems. However, as mentioned earlier, simply because an artificial preservative isn't on the label doesn't mean it isn't present in the food. It just means that the pet food manufacturer didn't add any *more*.
- **Moisteners.** Moisteners like propylene glycol, the main ingredient in antifreeze, are added to "chewy" foods. Moisteners have no benefit and may be harmful to your dog.
- **Artificial flavors or colors.** Even though these have been shown to be safe, remember that your dog probably eats dog food every day. Most artificial colors haven't been tested that thoroughly.
- **Artificial sweeteners.** Artificial sweeteners include corn syrup, sucrose, and ammoniated glycyrrhizin. This stuff just makes bad food taste good.

- **Meat or poultry (or "animal") by-products of unknown origin.** Although some meat by-products (like liver) are fine, others really have no function other than to fill up the package. Because the label doesn't tell you exactly what's in the can or package, you're better off avoiding the whole crowd of them. (Many people also charge that by-products aren't handled as carefully as whole-meat products.) Whole meats are the way to go unless you know what the by-products are. On the other hand, good beef by-products like liver may be *better* for your dog than processed "meal." It really is a tough call.
- **Generic brands.** They are generally much lower in quality than named brands.
- **Generic meat.** Choose food with the specific name of a meat (like beef, chicken, or turkey) as the first ingredient. Foods that just say "meat" or "poultry" should be avoided. Unfortunately, just because a product has beef as the first ingredient doesn't mean that the product is mostly beef. Some companies engage in a practice known as "splitting." If they can possibly do so, they will divide the cereal products up into separate categories, like "rice" and then "brown rice." Added together, there may be more rice than beef. But because the manufacturers are allowed to list them separately, beef is listed first.

Dry Food (Kibble)

Most kibble is largely corn, rice, or soybean based. Better brands contain meat or fish as the first ingredient, and while they cost more, they are actually a better bargain because your dog doesn't need to eat as much of it. Kibble is also more calorie-dense than canned dog food, as canned food contains a lot more water by volume. Large dogs like GSDs can actually have trouble getting their caloric needs met on a solely commercial canned food diet, which makes kibble a practical choice for many people.

Going Homemade

A good homemade diet can be more expensive than a cheap commercial dog food. This is especially true if you purchase human-grade, organically grown meat for your dog. But nutritionists who specialize in homemade diets say what you spend in the food market, you'll save at the vet.

Canned Food

Although some canned dog food smells unpleasant to humans (one reason most people prefer to serve kibble), most dogs prefer both the aroma and flavor of canned foods. In fact, some people serve such unappetizing dry fare that they have to anoint it with canned food before their dogs will touch it.

To find the best canned food for your GSD, check the label. Look for food containing whole meat, fish, or poultry as the first ingredient. Most lower quality canned foods have water as the first ingredient, and many canned foods are more than 78 percent water. The best canned foods use whole vegetables, not grain fractions like rice bran, rice flour, or brewers rice.

Unfortunately, the top canned foods can't often be found at the supermarket; you must go to the manufacturer, pet stores, or dog shows. This is because the high cost of shelf rental space in most supermarkets is out of the reach of many small, premium pet food manufacturers.

Semi-Moist Food

There is a variety of food labeled "semi-moist" that comes in little packages. Most of this food looks good, but nearly all of it is bad for your dog. Semi-moist food is loaded with sugar in the form of corn syrup and beet pulp (up to 25 percent). It is also made up of about 50 percent water. Your dog does not need this stuff, which promotes obesity and tooth decay. The shelf life of these products is also lower than either canned or dry food.

Homecooked Meals and Raw Diets

One healthy alternative to commercial foods is a home-cooked diet. In fact, it's quite possible to make a highly palatable, well-balanced meal for your dog at home. Of course, not every well-made homecooked meal will contain 100 percent of every nutrient your dog needs. It's also probable that not every single meal you eat will be "nutritionally balanced." Just follow the guidelines I list below and do your best.

Homemade food does not mean "table scraps," if you define that term as stuff that has gone bad and is ready to be thrown out. Bad food goes in the garbage. Good food goes in your dog. The best diets maintain nutritional balance by offering a rich variety of foodstuffs. Neither dogs nor humans need to have 100 percent of every nutrient in every meal. It's more important that both receive a diet high in variety and overall quality.

It is also true that preparing a healthy meal is more time consuming than plunking down a bowl of kibble. But there are ways to save time, such as cooking your dog's food at the same time you cook your own meals.

The greatest advantage of a homemade diet is that the power belongs to you, the dog owner. You control the ingredients. This is a great advantage for people who have dogs with health problems or multiple dogs with widely varying needs. If you decide to go the homemade route, be sure the diet provides the following:

- An animal-source protein. Unless your dog is allergic to all animal protein, a vegetarian diet is not normal and is not advised.
- A fat source, including essential fatty acids (EFAs).
- Adequate minerals, especially calcium, properly balanced with phosphorous.
- A supplement to provide vitamins and trace elements.

Many people feed their dogs raw food, and some claim it helps with allergies. This has not been my own experience. If you make your dog's food, cook it the same way you cook yours and for the same reasons: It's safer, it's more digestible, and it's more palatable. While most dogs can devour raw food and not become sick, in my opinion there's absolutely no point in taking the chance.

After a successful training exercise, reward your dog with small, healthy treats.

Treats

The simplest advice on treats that I can give is to go easy! The healthiest treats are bits of carrot or apple. You don't have to buy expensive biscuits filled with preservatives and dyes. For a special occasion, small chunks of cheese work perfectly.

Bones

Bones are naturally balanced sources of calcium and phosphorous, and dogs adore them. However, cooked bones are

dangerous, because they can easily splinter and damage your dog's throat and digestive system. The sterilized bones you can buy in the store are very dangerous in this regard; they are unnaturally hard and can cause broken teeth. Whole, *fresh* bones are safer, but the best choice is to have the bones thoroughly ground and cooked. Raw bones may carry bacterial dangers of their own, but the nutritional advantages are without par. It is important that the bones be both fresh and meaty for your dog to benefit. Start your dog off gradually, and watch him closely. Dogs need to learn to eat bones properly.

Your best choices are raw chicken legs and wings, because these bones have a perfect calcium/phosphorus ratio. Beef and even turkey bones may be too hard.

The most dangerous consequence of bone consumption is a perforated intestine, which allows toxins to escape into the dog's system. When dogs chew bones, they splinter, and splintering bones can puncture the esophagus or stomach. If you want to avoid these risks, give your German Shepherd Dog some safe chew toys instead, such as Nylabones.

Foods to Avoid

Grapes and Raisins

Reports have recently implicated large amounts of grapes and raisins (between 9 ounces and 2 pounds) in acute kidney failure in dogs, although no one knows exactly why. The kidney shutdown is so dramatic that aggressive treatment may be necessary to save your dog's life. Treatment for animals who have been poisoned by grapes and raisins includes:

- Administering activated charcoal. This helps prevent absorption of the toxic substance, whatever it is.
- Blood tests to evaluate kidney function.
- Hospitalization with intravenous fluids.

Chocolate

Chocolate, especially baker's chocolate, can cause a range of problems, including cardiovascular difficulties and even seizures.

Onions

A quarter cup of onions can induce hemolytic anemia, a severe but usually temporary condition. Serious cases can even require a blood transfusion. Garlic has the same properties, but garlic in very small amounts probably does your dog some good.

Corncobs

Some people think it's interesting to watch their dogs deal with corncobs. It's not. Dogs are not horses, and the cobs can mortally impact the intestines.

OBESITY

Obesity has become a growing concern in the dog population. In fact, as many as 25 percent of all dogs seen by veterinarians are overweight! Many causes exist, but primary among them is the sedentary lifestyle of the modern dog. In addition, feeding large numbers of table scraps, a poor diet, constant access to food, and competitive eating in multiple dog households may also contribute. In GSDs, common orthopedic conditions like hip dysplasia, osteoarthritis, cruciate ligament and meniscal injury, and osteochondrosis dissecans may reduce the exercise tolerance of the dog. Metabolic disorders including diabetes mellitus, hypothyroidism, hyperadrenocorticism (Cushing's disease), and hypoadrenocorticism (Addison's disease) may also play a part.

Obesity is associated with numerous health risks, including musculoskeletal problems, diabetes, and respiratory distress. By keeping your dog at the proper weight, you can "reduce" his age by years! If your dog is at his ideal weight, you should be able to feel and slightly see the outline of his ribs. His waist should be visible when viewed from above, and you should note a slight tuck of the abdomen when viewed from the side.

Feeding your German Shepherd Dog properly will enhance his life, improve his coat, boost his health, and make him a happier animal. And because you are in complete control of his diet, it's all in your hands!

GROOMING
Your German Shepherd Dog

The German Shepherd Dog is one of the "natural breeds." He does not require special clipping, combing, or scissoring. However, he does require regular and thorough brushing, as GSDs are heavy shedders.

Grooming should be a pleasant experience for both you and your GSD. It's a great way to bond with your dog while checking him for health problems. The best way to ensure this happens is to start when your dog is a puppy.

GROOMING SUPPLIES

Equipment you will need for grooming your GSD includes a wire slicker brush, pin brush, natural bristle brush, a shedding blade, mat breaker, metal rake for getting rid of shed hair, metal comb, scissors, nail clippers, towels, and shampoo. Basically, combs untangle hair, and brushes get rid of dead hair.

COAT CARE

Here's a tip: Start grooming your GSD with your hands! Before you ever take a comb or brush to him, a gentle massage (running your hands against the hair growth) will loosen dead hair, stimulate circulation, distribute oils, and make your dog happy!

Brushing

You can brush your GSD in under ten minutes, provided you do it regularly. The actual amount of time depends on the length of the coat. Although a long coat is considered a fault in the show ring, many German Shepherd Dogs do have longer coats, and they need longer and more frequent grooming sessions.

For best results, brush your GSD twice a week in order to manage the double coat. You'll need to work to remove the loose hairs—not just the hairs from the comparatively thin outer coat, but also the dense woolly hair from the undercoat. Believe me, this undercoat can be deceptively thick in some individuals, while others have comparatively little or none at all.

Use your brush, especially the wire slicker brush, with care. If you put too much

Shedding

This breed sheds all year round! Normal shedding is controlled by hormonal changes that are tied to a photoperiod (day length). It is also influenced by nutrition, general health, and stress. Many dogs lose their coats after surgery or whelping puppies.

downward pressure on it so that it rubs against the dog's skin, he may develop brush burns, or some small blood vessels might break. As you brush, angle the brush near the skin, not against it. Skin around the stomach, anus, and sheath is especially sensitive.

During times of heavy shedding, consider using a shedding blade. Use a shedding blade gently, with only the slightest pressure. Sometimes a lot of hair bulks up around the croup. This destroys the picture of the gently sloping croup. Use a mat breaker to thin the hair and loosen mats. Mats in the undercoat (especially common in the neck and thigh regions of some individuals) can be removed with a metal rake or shedding blade. This will massage the skin and distribute oils, as well as remove hair. If you want your GSD to look fluffier, with more coat volume, try first brushing the dog in the opposite direction of hair growth and then in the same direction of hair growth. (Use an ordinary bristle brush for this, not a slicker brush.)

Trimming

If the hair around the hocks is uneven or too long, you can trim it with thinning shears.

If there are any longer or stray hairs under the feet or between

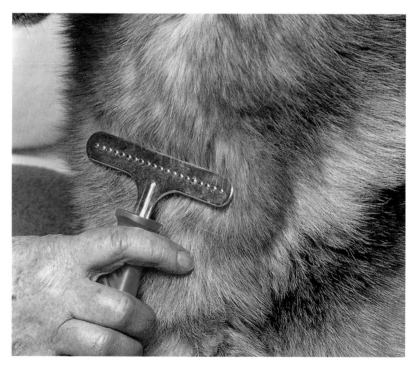

Shedding and slicker brushes should be used with care so as not to irritate your dog's skin.

the pads, scissor them out.

Some show groomers use a long-pinned pin brush on the tan-colored parts of the legs and brush in the opposite direction of hair growth. They then spray on mink oil, which gives the appearance of a darker red dog.

Bathing

You should bathe your dog about once a month. You can use a special canine shampoo or one meant for humans. The pH of a dog's skin is different from that of a person's skin, but there isn't any evidence that using a human shampoo is bad for your dog.

For most breeds, I recommend brushing before bathing, but unless your GSD is very matted, bathe him first. This is because when the coat is almost (but not quite) dry, you'll find that the loose hair comes out very easily.

Brushing your German Shepherd Dog twice a week will help you manage his double coat more effectively.

Start by making sure you have all of the needed supplies on hand, including shampoo, three or four old towels, and a rubber nonslip bathmat for the floor of the tub. You may want to place some cotton balls in your dog's ears to keep them dry. Water collecting in the ears just invites infection. However, don't forget they are in there! Although most dog shampoos are very mild, you may also want to apply mineral oil in the corners of your dog's eyes to protect them from shampoo irritation.

Invite (or carry) your dog into the tub and wet him down thoroughly. Use warm or tepid water. Apply the shampoo and rub into lather, keeping the soap out of his ears and eyes. Start shampooing at the top and neck, and work down and back.

If you don't like clipping your dog's nails, you can use a nail grinder, which will leave nail edges smooth.

Bathe the head last because when dogs get their heads wet, they shake. Rinse several times to prevent a dull coat and dry, flaky, or sticky skin.

As soon as the bath is done, begin drying him. In the winter, you may want to use a hand-held hair dryer, but in the summer you can let the dog air dry after you work him over with some fluffy towels (while he's still in the tub). Using a slicker brush in the direction of hair growth will also help during the drying process, because you can pretty much guarantee that more loose hair will be removed. Use a chamois cloth to bring out that final shine.

NAIL CARE

To clip your GSD's nails, you will need guillotine-type nail clippers, styptic powder, and files for trimming and finishing nails.

Try to clip your dog's nails regularly. A few dogs who exercise frequently on sidewalks or pavement keep their nails short naturally, but this is not usually the case. Most of the time, you'll need to clip the nails every three or four weeks. If you wait too long, the nails can grow into the pads. Even before this terrible state of affairs, dogs will find it hard to put their full body weight on feet with overlong nails, resulting in painful walking.

Most German Shepherd Dogs have black toenails, which are harder and denser than white nails.

Most GSDs have black toenails, which are harder and denser than white nails. Unfortunately, the black color makes the quick or vein in the nail impossible to see. Trim small amounts of the nail at a time, but do it regularly. The main concern is how much is too much! You don't want to remove the entire nail, of course. Dogs need their nails for work, and many show dogs have nails that are much too short. On the other hand, if you can hear your dog's nails "click" on the floor as he walks, it means they are too long.

Before you begin clipping, examine the toes for ingrown nails, soreness, redness, swelling, or discharges. These signs can signal serious trouble and mean you should take your dog to the vet. Assuming you are right-handed (for a leftie, just reverse, of course), place your left arm around the dog's middle and hold him against your chest. Speak firmly, but kindly. Hold the dog's foot in your left hand with your thumb on top of the toe and two fingers below on the paw pad. Insert the nail into the clipper, and clip quickly at about a 45 degree angle. It's better to make a few tiny clips than one big one if you can't see the quick. Many GSDs have dewclaws, the so-called fifth nail. Don't overlook these! In German Shepherd Dogs, the front dewclaws are usually left on, and the back ones are supposed to be removed. However, it is perfectly acceptable to remove the front ones as well.

You can minimize shedding by grooming your GSD regularly. In the winter, for example, many dogs develop dry skin and tend to shed more. Regular brushing will stimulate the dry skin and remove dead flakes and loose hairs.

If your dog's feet have been overlooked for a while, the sensitive quick may have grown out very close to the tip. If this is the case with your dog, first try filing the nail every day for about three weeks. It's almost impossible for nails to bleed from filing. Filing will encourage the quick to recede enough for you to start clipping. You may want to continue filing every day between clips until you can get the nails as short as they need to be.

If you make a mistake and clip the nail too short, use some styptic powder, flour, or cornstarch to staunch the bleeding. You can even stick the nail into a bit of bar soap! Hold with moderate pressure. After a minute or so, wipe away the excess powder and check the nail. If you don't take off the extra powder, it can harden into a kind of seal that will allow bleeding to start again when it breaks.

After clipping, file each nail so that it is smooth. (Don't file nails that have been clipped to the bleeding point, though.) Some people like to use a commercial nail polish or caps made just for dogs after grooming.

EAR CARE

Dogs have L-shaped ears, and all kinds of debris tend to collect in the corner of the L. Some waxy material may be present in normal ears, but if there is too much, it invites trouble. To remove this debris, fill your dog's ear canal with a good commercial ear cleaner. Ear cleaners should be slightly acidic but should not sting. (Avoid cleaners that contain alcohol.) Massage the base of the ear for 20 to 30 seconds to soften, loosen, and release the gunk in there. Then, wipe out the loose debris and excess fluid with a cotton ball

Your German Shepherd Dog's eyes should also be carefully inspected during the grooming process.

or soft cloth. Don't use a cotton swab, because that might pack the stuff farther down the ear canal. Repeat until you see no more debris. If the ears are really gunky, you may have to do this twice a day until everything is under control.

Speak gently to your dog and reward him for being good while you are cleaning his ears. After the ear is clean, let him shake his head, and allow some time for the ears to dry. Ear cleaning solutions usually contain a drying ingredient. However, if your dog has a ruptured or weakened eardrum, some ear cleansers and medications could be harmful.

In general, ear medications are applied after the ear is cleaned, but check with your vet.

You should inspect and clean your GSD's ears at least twice a week, especially if he swims or does a lot of rough work. Don't wait until your dog starts shaking his head! If the ears are swollen or red, it could be a sign that something is wrong. See Chapter 8 for more information.

EYE CARE

While the eyes don't have to be groomed the way the ears and teeth do, you should still inspect them during the grooming process. If they are red, cloudy, or have a green or yellow discharge, you should contact your veterinarian immediately.

DENTAL CARE

Brush your dog's teeth at least three times a week. If your dog is a puppy or has never had his teeth brushed before, start slowly. Many older dogs should have their teeth cleaned professionally

first so that you can start with a clean slate, so to speak.

Begin by just touching the muzzle and lifting the lips. Next, gently insert a finger to touch and stroke the teeth and gums. Then, introduce the toothpaste. Use only the edible kind specifically designed for dogs. Put a bit on your finger and let the dog sample the taste. Then, begin to apply it to the teeth and gums. When your dog allows you to touch all of his teeth with your finger, he is ready for a toothbrush!

When brushing, you can use either a circular motion or a sawing stroke—it doesn't really matter. The insides of the teeth are hard to reach, but luckily the tartar forms mostly on the outside anyway. Angle the brush at a 45 degree angle toward the gumline and brush away.

In addition to regular brushing, providing your dog with dental chews may also help keep his teeth in good condition. Nylabone makes some good chews that are suited to a German Shepherd's size and chewing power.

A well-groomed German Shepherd Dog is one of the most beautiful and elegant dogs in existence. A poorly groomed one is unhappy and unhealthy. You have it in your power to make sure your GSD belongs to the former, not the latter, category. A brush, a comb, some shampoo, and two minutes a day will turn your German Shepherd into the glorious, healthy, happy dog he was meant to be.

Take Care Everywhere

When grooming your GSD, pay special attention to the anal tissues. (Sorry, it's one of the joys of being a dog owner.) A swollen, red area or one with discharge means veterinary attention is required. If the area is matted with dried or compacted feces, soak it in warm water. (If you try to remove the fecal matter without soaking it, you could tear delicate tissues.) After cleaning, you may wish to apply a soothing lotion.

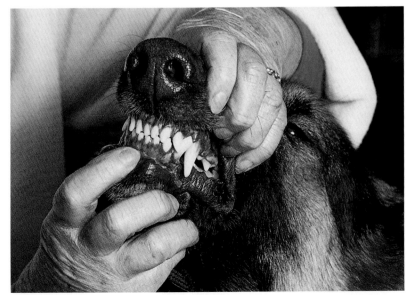

To accustom your dog to having his teeth brushed, begin by lifting the lips and touching the teeth and gums.

C h a p t e r

6

TRAINING AND BEHAVIOR

of Your German Shepherd Dog

Every German Shepherd Dog should be a trained German Shepherd Dog. This doesn't mean he needs to be a trained Schutzhund, but it does mean he should know and obey basic commands and act in a civilized way among company. Unfortunately, not all GSDs are trained GSDs. And even more unfortunately, their lack of training is not their fault. Rather, it is the fault of their owner. Fortunately, German Shepherd Dogs are almost infinitely trainable. They're just waiting for a teacher—you!

Training your dog is an ongoing process. As your dog matures, learns new skills, and adapts to a changing environment, he is constantly being challenged. No dog is ever finished training, just as no human is ever finished learning. This doesn't mean training has to be an unpleasant or onerous chore. On the contrary, training your dog is the best way to bond with him, interest him, and expose him to an exciting world. And because the German Shepherd Dog is undoubtedly the most versatile dog in the world, he has more opportunities for training adventures than almost any other breed.

Always remember that you are the leader of the pack, or family group. This is what your dog expects, and if you are not the leader, he may decide to take over. German Shepherd Dogs are not wimpy, and they have been bred to take control of sheep. This is why it's important not to be a sheep! For nonaggressive dogs, good obedience training is sufficient to make your dog understand that he is to be the follower, not the leader.

THE POWER OF POSITIVE TRAINING

The training I will emphasize in this book is positive reinforcement, usually in the form of food, petting, or praise, although some GSDs respond well to play as a reward. It's not the only kind of training that works, and it's not always best for every dog in every situation. However, it works most of the time for most dogs in most situations. No matter what kind of training program you choose, please don't hit, threaten, or hurt your dog. It really is counterproductive.

Avoid punishing your dog. Punishment simply doesn't work very well for animals. If you want your dog to behave well, he will need to internalize good behavior. Punishment makes

this difficult or impossible, because punishment is pain (either physical or psychological). Pain sets up barriers to internalization. For example, let's say a dog does something you don't like, such as snapping at a visitor. Yelling at or striking the dog creates an immediate unpleasant association in the dog's mind between the stimulus (the visitor) and the punishment. He will associate pain with visitors, and that will not make him like them any better.

SOCIALIZATION

German Shepherd Dogs are not highly social with strange dogs or strange people. This is their nature. In addition, some dogs become terribly frightened or aggressive toward other dogs, especially if they have ever been attacked. It only takes one incident to set up a lifetime of fear. Do not allow your dog to play with dogs of unknown temperament, such as those you might find in a dog park. The results could be unsettling, especially if your dog is young. Don't gamble that strange dogs are going to be kind to your puppy or that yours will be kind to someone else's. (I don't like dog parks myself, but I know they are a last resort for city dwellers who really have nowhere else to take their dogs.)

With that said, the necessity of carefully socializing your

Train Positive!

Severe, aversive, confrontational training methods were developed during World War II for training war dogs. You, on the other hand, will have much better results using praise and positive reinforcement. Your dog will like you better, and you will forge a bond of love and trust with him.

German Shepherd Dogs are extremely trainable, and a good trainer will help them achieve their fullest potential.

German Shepherd Dog from an early age cannot be stressed enough. To make your GSD more accepting of strangers in general, have him associate the arrival of visitors with fun or treats. When the visitor arrives, have her give the dog a treat. If possible, enlist the help of a friend to treat the dog, too. However, try to be realistic. The GSD has been bred to be a warning and guard dog. He is not an Irish Setter, so don't expect him to act like one. Your GSD will continue to be reserved around strangers, but that

Carefully socializing your GSD from an early age to other dogs and people is critical to his emotional development.

doesn't mean he will be aggressive. These are very responsive and obedient dogs. Once he understands what you want, he will do it.

Try to walk your German Shepherd Dog every day for a minimum of 30 minutes, even if it's cold or raining. This is in addition to other exercise, since a leisurely walk a couple of times a day is nothing for a GSD! But walking your dog on a leash gives him a chance to meet new people and get critical social interaction. Walking your dog also gives you a chance to work on simple obedience exercises like sitting and heeling.

HOUSETRAINING

Let's start with the basics. Before search and rescue, service work, agility, or flyball comes housetraining.

Dogs develop their elimination patterns during the first few months of their lives, and one rule they all agree on is that it's best not to eliminate where they sleep. Once they find a spot they like, they will return to it.

The first rule of housetraining is to get a crate. You can call it a kennel or a cage or even a carrier, but get one, either plastic or wire. Used properly, crates are not cruel, and they provide a safe haven for your dog. Crates can become cruel when dogs are shoved into

If you want your GSD to eliminate on schedule, feed him on schedule.

them for countless hours at a time, but that is not a proper use. When housetraining your puppy, he should be in the crate anytime he is not supervised by you. He will learn that the crate is a good place if you start feeding him in it. Say, "Kennel!" in a happy tone and put his food inside. (If it's not mealtime, you can use a food treat.) After he begins to associate food with the kennel, only treat him randomly. This is what dog trainers call "variable reinforcement," and it works better (as well as being more convenient) than always using a food treat. This is a general principle you should carry into other kinds of training as well. Start with consistent rewards, and then switch to variable ones.

If your dog cries in the kennel, ignore the noise. Do not give in and let him out—in that case, you will find he is training you.

Keys to Successful Housetraining

The keys to successful housetraining include:

- Crate
- Reward
- Attention
- Patience
- Scheduling

Crate

If your dog accepts his crate as his sleeping den, he will be less likely to use it as a toilet. Dogs simply don't like to eliminate where they sleep. Of course, you can't keep your dog in a crate longer than his bowels and bladder can stand! Remember that puppies have tiny bladders, and their sphincters are insufficiently developed to hold waste for a long period of time. You should never keep a puppy in a crate for more than two hours except at night, when he is supposed to be sleeping anyway. Confining a dog for long periods in a crate is extremely detrimental to his physical and emotional health. Sooner or later, he will start eliminating in the crate out of necessity—and if he doesn't, he may be well on his way to developing bladder stones.

Reward

Always reward your puppy, or for that matter, an untrained older dog, with praise or a treat when he eliminates outdoors. If he responds to praise, that's best. Make the praise overwhelming—

jump for joy! Let him know that you are thrilled with his behaviors. Another treasured reward is a walk. Some people take their dog out, let him eliminate, and then immediately bring him back inside. As a result, the message he is getting is that as soon as he eliminates, it's time to go back in the house. This may cause him to try to hold it as long as possible, potentially resulting in accidents indoors.

As an alternative, give your dog a walk or a play session as soon as he's successful. If you do take him out for a long walk and don't get a result, try bringing him indoors and then immediately taking him out again. He may have forgotten his duties during the excitement of the walk and won't remember until he's inside again. Most importantly, never punish your dog for making a mistake. Don't yell at him, strike him, or rub his nose in his mistake. These practices are cruel and ineffective.

Attention

Your dog will give you signals that he needs to go out, but it's up to you to figure out what they are. Sometimes, a dog will do something refreshingly obvious like actually going to the door. But don't expect that, at least not at first. It's more likely that your dog will give you subtle signs that he has to go, like licking his lips, circling, looking puzzled, or if you're really lucky, actually whining. The instant you notice these signals, grab the leash and take him out. Don't simply put the dog out and hope all will be well. Go out with him so that you can praise his success.

Putting your puppy on a regular feeding and elimination schedule will help him become housetrained.

Patience

You wouldn't expect to toilet train a child in a week, so don't expect your German Shepherd Dog to be reliable after only a few days, either. He is a baby with weak sphincter muscles and a small bladder. By properly using the crate, watching your dog like a hawk, and keeping to a schedule, you'll encourage the proper response from him. But a puppy will inevitably make

Exercising your dog before training may help work off some of his excess energy.

some mistakes. If you don't find these mistakes until after the fact, simply clean them up without comment. If you catch the puppy in the act, scoop him up, tuck his tail between his legs (this helps prevent "spillage"), and say, "Out!" or "Quick!" Don't say, "No!" "No" is a negative word, and your puppy may think that eliminating is wrong, no matter where he does it. If he gets that idea, he'll start hiding it from you.

Schedule

Dogs not only like routine, but it's also good for them. Put your puppy on a regular feeding and elimination schedule as soon as possible. The more regular the schedule, the easier it will be to housetrain your dog. This may mean you will have to take some time off from work or hire a puppy sitter during the housetraining process, which usually takes about two weeks if you do everything right. This may seem extreme, but believe me, it makes all the difference. Your puppy will usually need to eliminate after naps, after meals, after playtime, first thing in the morning, and last thing at night. You'll probably have better luck if you give your puppy his last meal around six o'clock in the evening. If you feed him any later than that, you'll be getting up later that night to take him out.

Different dogs have different schedules. You may have one who needs to go out when you're eating, when you are taking a shower, when you're on a conference call, or during the most thrilling moments of your favorite television show. However, this is all part of the joy of owning a German Shepherd Dog!

When Accidents Occur

If your puppy does have an accident on the carpet, dilute the spot with a dampened cloth. Then, clean the area with a bacteria/enzyme digester available at your local pet supply, grocery, or hardware store. These get rid of both the stain and the smell. The latter is very important; even if you can't smell the urine, your dog can, and he will only be encouraged to use the spot again. For best results, make sure you use enough of the product to penetrate both the carpet and the pad underneath. Leave it on for the required length of time. Enzyme digesters work very well, but they are not quick fixes. After you put down the solution, cover the area with plastic and step on it a few times to ensure the spot is well saturated. Keep the plastic in place so the digester doesn't dry out. (Never use an ammonia product to clean up dog urine. It smells like urine to dogs and will only encourage them to use that spot again.)

As sheep tenders, German Shepherd Dogs are by nature highly alert dogs, extremely tuned to even the slightest changes in their environment. They will react to these changes, a quality that makes them highly trainable.

BASIC TRAINING

Before you begin any kind of training, make sure your dog is physically well. It's also imperative that everyone in the family makes a commitment to be on board with the training program you have chosen. This includes children, who should be supervised while helping with the training.

Wait until you are in a calm and relaxed mood to work with your dog. GSDs are psychic when it comes to picking up on

Training Goals

Keep your goals clear and realistic while you're training your dog. Not every GSD is a Rin Tin Tin, believe it or not, although every GSD can be trained. While environment is critically important for any dog, the fact is that after puppyhood, a dog's essential temperament is set. Training will not transform a shy, anxious, submissive dog into a super-confident hero. It also won't make a dominant dog submissive. However, good training will make the most of what your dog comes equipped with!

It is so much easier to prevent a problem than to solve one. And that's what training is all about. You can't train your dog until you know what you want from him. Make a list of everything reasonable you would like your dog to do or not do on command. Then, set up regular training sessions, each with a specific goal. If you have no goal, you won't know whether or not you've accomplished anything. Keep a log of your training sessions, and write down at the top of the page what your goal is for each session. Afterward, record how the session went.

moods, and your dog's mood will echo yours. If you want your dog to associate training with happiness, you have to be happy.

You may also want to exercise your dog before training to take a little of the edge off. Your energetic, life-loving GSD has a lot to occupy his mind. After exercise, practice in a quiet, restricted area where neither of you will be distracted or able to run away (even though you both might feel like it).

Don't try training your dog right before dinnertime—his mind will be on other things. A hungry dog cannot keep his mind on training.

When asking your dog to do something, use clear, one- or two-word commands, not full sentences. Your dog is smart, but syntax is beyond him. And unless you are calling your dog to come, don't use his name as part of the command. Practice training inside the house and outside. You want to choose a place that will allow your dog to succeed!

Only train your dog when you are relaxed and calm. Waiting until the dog makes a disastrous mistake and then saying angrily, "Well, I'm going to stop that behavior right now!" is a recipe for failure. Wait until you are calm, figure out the problem, and then go to work on it.

Finally, put yourself in your dog's place. Think about how you like being taught. If you don't enjoy being yelled at, yanked around, or frightened, assume that your dog doesn't either. A kind,

Choosing a Training Collar

Owners have a multitude of collar choices: buckle, choke, prong, head halters, and even harnesses (which aren't strictly collars at all). There are also varieties of each of these. You will find that each dog responds to each kind of collar individually, so you will need to experiment to find what's right for your GSD. In general, I recommend that you begin with a plain buckle collar. With the right kind of positive reinforcement training, it's all you'll ever need.

If you decide you would like to do formal obedience, check the AKC rules to see which collars are "legal," and which aren't. Generally speaking, only buckle collars and choke collars are allowed, although the rules seem to be subject to interpretation.

Many people recommend the use of halter-type collars. These are wonderful devices. They are much more effective than traditional collars, and they are gentler as well. Although they take some adjustment and getting used to by you and your dog, I think you'll be pleased with the result. The bigger and stronger your GSD, the more effective you will find them.

The choice of collar finally depends on you, your dog, and your training method, as what works for one dog may not work for another.

patient, gentle approach will yield better results and strengthen the bond between you.

Watch Me

This is the basic focus command. If your dog isn't paying any attention to you, he won't be able to learn anything. Help him focus by using positive reinforcements and treats. This doesn't mean that you should give your dog food every time he looks at you. It means that he should always consider it as a viable possibility. Once he learns that "watch me" brings praise or even a reward, he'll be anxious to learn what you have to say next.

To teach "watch me," say the words and hold a treat near your

"Come" is one of the most important commands in basic training.

face. If your German Shepherd Dog doesn't see the treat at first, you may have to start to lower it toward his field of vision. He'll catch on soon. Although the number of times you do anything should depend on the age, training, and maturity of your GSD, you should stop while he is still having fun. Usually a minute or two is long enough.

Come

This is one of the most important of all commands. If there is one thing that you'd like your dog to do reliably every time, this is it. Dogs who don't come on command are annoying at the least, and at the worst, they are in serious danger. If you fail here, your puppy may turn "come" into a game, in which your part of the game is to call him, and his part of the game is to see how long he makes you stand there looking silly. I should warn you, however, that it is always possible for even the best behaved dog not to come when called if something more interesting is moving in the opposite direction. None of us is perfect.

When you first begin teaching the command, wait until the dog is already heading in your direction and then call him. It's important to wait until the dog is already headed in your direction; don't initiate the command yourself. If he suddenly stops, call him again and use a small treat to lure him. When he gets to you, give him lots of praise, attention, or even a treat. The key is to look sharp and be prepared to call "Come" in a cheerful tone every time you see your dog doing it anyway. If your dog happens not to obey, don't chase him. Turn your back and walk in the opposite direction. He'll probably come to you. When he does, give him a treat and start walking again. The key is to make him think that coming to you and being by your side is the most rewarding activity there is.

The biggest mistake people make is thinking the dog has learned the command after just a few tries. It takes repeated, long-term application to make it sink in. Sessions should last approximately 15 minutes.

Make sure your German Shepherd Dog has access to plenty of fresh, cool water while participating in training exercises.

No

Right up there with the come command is the no command. "No" means "Desist immediately!" You may combine it with a reference to what he's doing wrong: "No chew!" means "Stop eating that; it's my prom dress." Some people think that saying no is cruel, but it is actually quite the contrary. "No" is simply a guide to correct behavior.

"No" is a mysterious word to dogs unless you utter it immediately in conjunction with the forbidden behavior. You can't walk into a room five minutes after the doilies were devoured, shake one in the dog's face, and shriek, "No! No!" At that point, he will have forgotten what he's done wrong and wonder why you're yelling at him. If your dog is chewing something inappropriate,

Sprechen Sie Deutsche?

While German Shepherd Dogs can learn any language with ease, it's fun to teach them commands in their "native" German! You will amaze and confound your friends with your dog's linguistic skills (and improve your own as well). Here are some of the most common training expressions used in German:

Come: *Hier*

Down: *Platz*

Fetch: *Bring*

Good dog: *Braver Hund*

Heel: *Fuss*

Leave it: *Lass es*

No: *Nein*

Out: *Aus*

Sit: *Sitz*

Speak: *Gib laut*

Stay: *Bleib*

say, "No chew" while he's engaged in the behavior and hand him something more acceptable. Then, praise him. This way, you won't confuse your dog or destroy his ego.

Off

This means, "Get the heck off the couch, Arthur! How many times have I told you not to sit on the couch?" You can also use "no" to make him get down, but "off" is better because it is more specific. It tells the dog exactly what you want him to do right now.

More dominant dogs should be lured with a treat and praised for obedience. In fact, always reward a dominant animal for submissive behavior. In some cases, you may have to attach a leash to the dog in order to get him to come down.

To reinforce the message, you can teach your dog both "up" and "off." That's one way to let him know that furniture is by invitation only. Both commands can be taught the same way, by using treats or other rewards.

Give It and Drop It

These commands are not identical, and a well-trained dog knows both of them. After all, you may want your GSD to give you the stick he has so unexpectedly retrieved for you, but you'd rather he just dropped the rotten rabbit he dug up. It is good practice for you to be able to remove anything your dog has in his mouth without a protest from him.

The easiest way to make a dog drop what he has in his mouth is to offer him a tastier alternative. Luckily, at first, puppies are

Mixed Messages

Many people seem to have more trouble learning the meaning of "no" than their dogs do. When saying no, you must not betray your verbal command by virtue of your tone or body language. If you say no but are secretly thinking, "Oh, it's so adorable the way he ate my slippers," he'll know you don't really mean it. Next time, he'll eat your more expensive running shoes.

usually likely to pick up a nonedible item that isn't really that interesting, like an old shoe. He will probably release the item immediately if offered something better and told to drop it. You will want to practice this command with low-value items first. Practicing with tug-of-war is a good way to make him learn the command. (Contrary to what is sometimes said, there is nothing wrong with playing tug-of-war, or even letting your GSD win. The key is that *you* decide who wins.) Of course, if he selects a high-value, dangerous item (like a rotten rabbit), you may have to put on gloves and just take it. However, be sure to reward him for it. Never allow the dog to have anything you don't want him to.

"Give it" is a command used to get something placed directly in your hand. The main difference between "drop it" and "give it" is that with the latter command, you are asking him to put it in your hand. (You should hold it out as a signal.) Practice by handing the dog something he doesn't want to hold in his mouth all that much anyway. As you hand it to him, say, "Give it" immediately, and praise or treat him when he lets it drop, as he probably will. Gradually increase the value of the object and the consequent reward. Soon, he should drop whatever he has into your hand upon your command.

Sit

This is the easiest and most popular of all commands to teach. Simply say, "Sit," and hold a treat slightly above your dog's eye level. This will encourage him to sit down. Praise him lavishly when he succeeds. Be careful to praise him as he *sits,* not when he starts to get up. When you do want your dog to rise, give him a release command such as "break." Some trainers use "okay," but because people use that word constantly in regular conversation, it's

too easy for a dog to misunderstand. Training sessions should last no longer than five minutes.

Stay

Although some people teach the stay as a separate command, I prefer to use the sit, which means that my dog should sit until I say, "Okay!" I believe that teaching the stay as a separate command is confusing to dogs, because you're not asking them to do anything new—you're just asking them to keep doing what you have already asked them to do. However, other people believe that saying "Stay" signals to the dog early that he'll be sitting for quite some time. At any rate, never ask your dog to sit-stay for more than a few seconds when you are starting out. You want to make success easy for him.

Teach stay by saying the word and slowly retreating. Reward him for remaining in one place. Again, quit while the training is still fun. The length of time you teach this command depends on your individual dog, but five minutes is usually long enough.

When training your dog, use tiny food treats as a reward. These should be something like tiny bits of cheese or freeze-dried liver that can be swallowed quickly without chewing.

Down

This command should be taught after the sit command. While your GSD is sitting, take a treat and hold it in front of his face, lowering it slowly to the ground. The dog should follow suit. If he doesn't, keep him in a sitting position and very slowly pull the treat forward in front of him close to the ground. He'll have to lie down to reach it. Praise him when he succeeds. Dogs have to trust you on this one, as lying down makes them feel vulnerable. Don't try it until you and your pooch have established a strong bond. Training sessions should last from five to ten minutes.

Teach stay by saying the word and then gradually retreating.

Heel

A correctly heeling dog is a pleasure to walk. The trouble involved in training him to move quietly at your side will be more than made up for later, when you are walking your dog with one hand, holding the baby/book bag/dog show trophy in the other. If you have a puppy, take heart. A puppy is much easier to teach to heel than an older dog. He naturally wants to come with you, and he usually has no bad habits to unlearn.

Use a 6-foot nylon or leather lead for heel training exercises. Never use a chain leash, because it is too heavy and noisy. Also, don't wrap the leash around your hand. It's a less effective instrument that way. Besides, you could hurt your hand if the dog lunges at something. If your dog works well on a plain leather collar, use that. The less control you need, the more pleasurable the exercise will be for both of you. It's always best if you have accustomed your dog to walk happily at your side before attaching a leash to him, and you can easily do this with the use of treats. Simply hold the treat at your side in about the same position you'll want his head to be when he is heeling. If you are both successful with this method, the leash will become an afterthought!

"Down" should be taught after your GSD has successfully learned how to sit.

It's traditional for dogs to heel at the left side of their owners, but there's no law about it. Lefties may prefer walking their dogs on the right side. However, if you're planning on showing your dog in conformation or obedience, it's best to use the customary left side. Begin by reaching out and touching your dog. He will probably look up at you expectantly, which is good. You must get him to pay attention to you and keep his eye on you. Say, "Fido, heel," and begin walking. Keep his chest in line with your knee, and don't allow him to lead. During a heeling exercise, stop at every curb. This is good practice for both of you, as you don't want your dog to get the idea that it's all right to run across the street. When you are finished, loosen the lead completely and say, "Break." This is the signal that your dog may now sniff around and be doggish to his heart's content.

Some dogs pull at the leash, also known as forging. Forging begins long before you have attached the lead to the collar. It begins when your dog sees the lead. If you can't control him at this point, don't expect that the upcoming foray will be a walk in the park, even if it is a walk in the park. Have your dog sit or stand quietly while you attach the lead. Do not put the lead on while he's dancing around. In fact, insist that he remain calm. If he starts jumping around when it's on, take the lead off and calmly begin again. He will soon learn that the only way he's getting out the door is quietly. Otherwise, you will have a struggle on your hands before the walk even begins.

Please Leave

I use this command to remove my dogs from the kitchen, especially when I am cooking or dining. Actually, I say, "Aroint thee, beast!" but they get the picture. To teach "leave," take your dog's collar and remove him to the desired room. Then, praise him. When he comes back, say, "Please leave," and repeat. Do this until he gets the message. You may use treats to explain further.

FORMAL TRAINING

Not all training is equal. First, training comes in various types. The most basic is obedience training (sit, stay, come, down, off, and heel). In more advanced training, your dog will learn how to retrieve objects or perform specific duties. There is even athletic training, which will help your dog compete in sports like agility or flying disc. Lastly, there's behavior modification training, which helps owners manage or change unacceptable behaviors such as aggression or separation anxiety.

Sometimes calling in the help of an expert is a great idea, especially with a high-performing dog like a German Shepherd Dog. The key is finding a good one. The most important thing is to find someone whose training philosophy makes sense to you. If it doesn't, you won't be able to follow through on your own afterward. After all, the trainer is not going to just be training your dog—she is going to be showing *you* how to train your dog. There is a training option called "day training," in which you drop your dog off at a

Learning to Heel

The heeling exercise is not a potty break. Don't allow your dog to stop, lag, lunge ahead, or smell the roses while training. Every once in a while, however, after a successful heel, you can take a mini break from training. Again, signify the break clearly by loosening the leash while saying, "Break" or something similar. Then, you can allow your dog to sniff around, but he should never be permitted to pull.

A good trainer will explain her methods and allow you to observe her in action.

training center and pick him up later (kind of like doggie day care and often, in fact, run by the same people). This is an excellent opportunity for busy owners, but you'll still have to reinforce at home what your dog learned in school.

The trainer will help you set and achieve realistic goals. After all, your dog will not go from a juvenile delinquent to Rin Tin Tin in six easy lessons, but he should make definite progress toward good behavior and obedience. In addition, the trainer will be able to use various approaches if the first one doesn't work. Dogs are like children; each one learns differently, and sometimes you have to experiment a bit before you find a method that works.

A good trainer will be able to explain her philosophy and give you a chance to see how she trains. She will also never tell you that your dog is hopeless. Most good trainers also have certification and education in dog training.

After you start to work with the new trainer, observe your dog. Does he seem to enjoy the sessions, or does he become nervous and anxious at the sight of the trainer? If the latter is true, something is definitely wrong and you should consider finding a new trainer.

You can find training programs by calling your local shelter, kennel club, or vet.

Formal Training Options

Nowadays, you have many options for professionally training your dog. You can choose between individual and group lessons, and you also have the option of having someone come to your home or taking your dog somewhere outside of the home.

Group lessons are not only the least expensive, but they are also the best option for most people and their dogs. First, they provide support. You can learn just from watching others. Second, they provide a great chance for socializing your dog. This is something that is very important for German Shepherd Dogs, as they are not naturally the chummiest of pets. Their natural protective instincts come readily into play, so you can use training classes as an opportunity to teach your dog that social occasions are fun, not threatening.

Dogs who really detest other dogs or who have trouble focusing, however, do better with individual lessons. Private lessons allow you to focus more intensely on your dog's problems, and they give you more chances to ask questions. They also let the trainer completely tailor her lessons to your dog's particular needs, and training will proceed at your dog's pace—you won't have to struggle to keep up with the class or be held back because the Basset Hound in the class refuses to do anything. The big disadvantage of private lessons, of course, is cost, which can run about four times what group lessons cost.

PROBLEM BEHAVIORS

The first thing to remember about a problem behavior is that for you it's a problem. For the dog, it's a reaction to a completely different problem that he is experiencing. For example, let's say a dog is lonely or bored. That is his problem. His solution might be to chew something, which you see as the problem. However, this action happens to relieve his tension, and it provides him with something to do. It's a fact that every "problem" dog behavior is, for the dog, a solution to a problem.

Training the Older Dog

Older dogs not only can be taught new tricks—it's good for them! Although older dogs may be a bit slower on the uptake, learning new things helps keep them alert. Just as with a puppy, use a food treat to teach him to sit, lie down, or cease barking. The better the treat, the more effect it will have! Old-timers may be blasé about a dog biscuit, but a bit of cheese will get their attention. Included with the treat, of course, is his cue word. (You may have to speak very clearly.) Your dog will soon associate the word and the treat and comply with your command.

Even if the training doesn't really accomplish anything, your dog will enjoy the time spent with you and the attention you are lavishing on him.

Beware the Stare

In dog language, a stare equals a challenge. Domestic dogs have learned to put up with us rudely staring at them, but it's a fairly unnatural adjustment, and they have to keep remembering we are not hostile beings. The best thing to do with a dominant dog is to stare at the tip of his ear. You have the advantage of looking at the dog, but in his mind you are not actually issuing a challenge.

Fortunately, there are some adjustments that you can make that will help you and your dog live together in harmony:

1. **Change your behavior.** It may be that you are doing something, consciously or unconsciously, to produce the behavior you are trying to correct. For example, cuddling a frightened dog is guaranteed to reinforce the fearful behavior. It's easier to train yourself than to train your dog, anyway.

2. **Change your dog's behavior.** This may include teaching him to accept baths, obey basic commands, release toys and food, and so forth. Naturally, to get your dog to behave differently, you will probably have to do something different yourself.

3. **Build a higher fence, confine the dog, etc.** Some canine behaviors are so ingrained that it may be impossible to train the dog out of them. If you can't retrain, you must restrain.

4. **Medicate the dog.** Some bad behavior has a medical cause. If this is the case, it may have a medical solution.

5. **Medicate yourself.** Perhaps a nice cup of herbal tea will put you in a better temper.

6. **Get used to it.** This seems a bit harsh, but sometimes it's easier for everyone concerned. If your dog has a minor problem behavior that doesn't lend itself to any of the above treatments, just ignore it.

One size does not fit all. The cure that works depends on the target behavior, its cause, and your patience. The important thing to remember is that most inappropriate dog behaviors are "fixable." Consistent training (routines are great!), fair leadership, and patience are the keys. As leader, you are the one to make the decisions, control the resources (like food and attention), and set the boundaries. It's mostly common sense, especially if you stop once in a while to think, "How does my dog perceive what I am doing?"

Let's look at a few of the more common problems GSD owners may face and at least some of the ways to deal with them.

Aggression

Aggression is violence or the threat of violence. Dogs use dominance to find their place in the order of things. Left to their own devices, they even exhibit a substantial amount of actual aggression among themselves. In civilized society, however, we frown on such behavior, especially when it's directed against ourselves or other pets. All signs of such aggression must be taken seriously.

Canine aggression against people is a growing problem, with reported dog bites increasing at the rate of 2 percent annually. According to the American Veterinary Medical Association, almost 4.5 million dog bites occur every year, and 334,000 of them are serious enough to warrant emergency room treatment. About 2 million children are bitten annually, half of them under the age of twelve. In fact, half of all children twelve and younger have been bitten by dogs. Sixteen to 20 people are killed every year by dogs. The fault lies in irresponsible breeding and irresponsible ownership (not just in the United States but worldwide), but it has become a problem for everyone.

Bold, dominant dogs tend to hold their heads high; submissive dogs bow their heads. They also recognize the same posture in your own body language. Approach a dog with your head high and you exude dominance; lower it and you appear submissive (or as if you are eliciting play).

An aggressive German Shepherd Dog is a very dangerous dog! Between 1979 and 2001, GSDs were involved in over 40 human fatalities in the United States, including 7 adults, 24 children aged one through ten, and nine babies under the age of one year. Careful studies, however, reveal details that suggest the dog is not always to blame. In fact, some of the fatalities resulted from attacks by on-duty and off-duty police dogs, while others were caused by extreme owner negligence.

Some insurance companies will no longer write coverage for people owning German Shepherd Dogs. I tell you this not to frighten you out of owning one of these beautiful and intelligent animals but to remind owners that this is a powerful animal that can be dangerous in the wrong hands.

Dogs become aggressive for three reasons:

1. **They are stressed.** Dogs become stressed when they are hurt or afraid, or when they feel their dominance, possessions (including puppies), food, or territory is being threatened.
2. **They are hunting prey, such as rabbits, cats, or smaller dogs.** This is an inbred kind of aggression that is practically impossible to train a dog out of.
3. **They are following orders.** This is the aggression characteristic of a trained Schutzhund, and it is a behavior that can be initiated and halted immediately by a competent owner. (I once knew a GSD police dog who was so ill-trained that he would bite anyone who came near him, including the veterinarian, with the exception of his handler! This was bad training.)

It is the first kind of aggression that gives owners the most trouble, because it is often owner-directed. In many cases, this kind

Your GSD and Others

Even dogs who accept rough behavior from a child in the family may not put up with it from a neighbor's child or a visitor. It is your responsibility to monitor your dog's interactions with others.

of aggression occurs against "soft" owners who have simply failed to make their dogs understand who is in control. This kind of aggression is often not "solved" by simple obedience classes, either. Obedience does not get at the root of the problem (and for some dogs actually increases stress). Many aggressive dogs do beautifully in obedience—they sit, lie down, heel, and fetch on command. Then, when they get home, they still show aggression when their owners attempt to remove them from the couch. Unneutered males between the ages of eighteen months and three years are most likely to express this kind of aggression. Male dogs often seek, even if only briefly, to achieve alpha position. In dog language, the alpha dog is the top dog in the pack. They are really just as happy to lose, but many will make the effort just for form's sake. Obviously, this is an important time to assert your dominance.

Solution

Dogs may experience stress from a variety of life changes, and they may try to fill the gap that has opened in the domestic leadership structure. Dogs may suddenly become dominant, or in rare cases, aggressive toward a lower-status family member, usually a child. If your dog is bossy toward some members of the family only, those persons should take over feeding and training the dog. They need to establish clearly to the animal that they are alpha over him. Obedience training is also essential. On the other hand, never allow your child to pester a dog. If the dog walks away from a child, it means he doesn't want to be bothered anymore. A more subtle indication of displeasure is the stiffening of the animal's body when he's being petted. A growl is an even stronger hint. Your child should be taught to recognize and heed these signals.

Obviously, no biting or aggressive behavior should be tolerated or ignored. If you make excuses for your dog, the situation will only get worse. If your dog does bite a person, do not physically punish him, although you should express your disapproval in a stern voice and remove the dog from the situation instantly. Striking a dog will only add fear to the complex factors that induced the bite, and this will increase the odds that he will bite again. You should get him to a professional trainer or veterinary behaviorist specializing in aggressive behavior.

Certain kinds of aggressive behavior respond well to drug therapy. Clinicians use antidepressants, sedatives and tranquilizers, hormonal therapy, and antianxiety drugs to work with aggressive dogs. Trainers have also been experimenting with holistic remedies for aggression. Herbs like St. John's Wort, valerian, and hops have a soothing effect on dogs, and certain flower essences (snapdragon, for instance) may be useful in conjunction with training.

Dietary changes, such as switching to a low-protein dog food with no additives, are helpful in some cases. Lots of exercise is important, too, if only because the dog becomes too tired to pick a fight. It also channels his energy into more constructive paths.

Barking

Barking comes as naturally to a dog as talking does to us. For both species, barking and talking are forms of communication. When a dog barks, he's telling the attentive listener the following:
- He's there
- How far away he is and in what direction
- How excited/happy/mournful/bored he is

Dogs seem to bark differently at the approach of friends, strangers, and enemies, and many alert dog owners claim to know the difference. In fact, barking can mean anything from a threat of attack to an invitation to play, and should be read along with other body language cues. Volume, intensity, pitch, and duration all give subtle clues to meaning.

Solution

It does no good to yell, scream, or spray water at a barking dog. These methods merely make him bark more. Likewise, aversive "training" collars that deliver a shock, citronella mist, or noise to a barking dog are ineffective and cruel. (Even citronella, the least objectionable of the "training" collars, makes some dogs sick, while others just ignore it.) Once you start relying on these devices, you're stuck with them. The dog will continue to bark whenever he's not wearing the collar or sees that you have no squirt bottle in hand. You can handle the situation much better with a response that does not depend on fear or punishment for its effectiveness.

If your dog barks to warn you of visitors, that's fine. Praise him for the barking, and reassure him that all is well. If he continues to bark, ignore him until he stops. If your dog is barking to request something like treats or going for a run, deny the privilege until the dog ceases to bark, and then reward quiet behavior. If your GSD is

Too Chewy

If your older dog suddenly begins chewing, he may have dental or upper gastrointestinal difficulties. This is definitely a problem that needs to be addressed, because the chewing can become habitual, even after the initial problem goes away. If you suspect that your dog's chewing habit is caused by a medical problem, consult your veterinarian.

barking because he's excited to be outside, bring him in the second he starts. He'll soon learn that barking results in being brought in the house.

Digging

Digging is a natural activity for dogs. They dig to find cool places to rest in the summer, to hunt for little animals in the ground, to prepare a nest, and just for something to do when they're bored. Unfortunately, this natural behavior can turn your lawn into a minefield.

To discourage your dog from chewing inappropriate objects, provide him with suitable chew toys.

Solution

You have several approaches when it comes to digging, all of which involve management. First, you can encourage your dog to dig where you want him to by supplying him with an "earthbox," which is simply a child's sandbox filled with attractive, soft, diggable earth or play sand. You can encourage him to dig in it by hiding one of his more precious toys there. You can also restrict your dog's access to valuable real estate with a fence. If this is not practical, simply watch him like a hawk and put him in the earthbox, perhaps with a great toy anchored to it to encourage his presence. However, you should never punish your dog for doing what comes naturally.

If your GSD digs inside the house, he may be looking for mice or other home invaders. It's also common for dogs to dig at new carpeting. The new material hasn't yet absorbed the familiar odors of the house, and your dog might dig at it to find out just what this strange new stuff is made of. You'll need to keep your dog separated from the new material until the carpet has absorbed familiar household odors. Some kinds of digging is nesting behavior, too. If associated with other aberrant behavior, it might be an emotional problem. Usually, though, digging is just normal behavior.

Chewing

Like digging, chewing is a normal behavior for dogs. Dogs can't be expected to know what is appropriate unless you teach them. However, sometimes it crosses the line into destructive behavior. The only sure solution is to crate your dog or separate him from valuable property when you are unable to supervise him. Punishing him, though, is wrong and doesn't work anyway. It may be a temptation to hit the roof when you come home to find your living room in shreds, but doing so will only make your GSD associate your return with something awful, because he has no idea why you're angry with him. Dogs must be caught in the act to make the connection between inappropriate behavior and your displeasure.

Although your GSD may chew things for many reasons, including playfulness and boredom, he does not do it for revenge. The link between ripping up the couch and getting even with his owner is too tenuous and silly for dogs.

Too Noisy?

In the United Kingdom, legal action may be taken against the owner of a noisy dog under the Environmental Protection Act 1990, Section 80.

Solution

Unfortunately, many dogs regard any attention as better than no attention. It will take some self-control on your part not to respond to negative behavior with negative attention. But you must. Remove the target item (or the dog) with the minimum amount of fuss. Give him plenty of loving attention when he is behaving himself, not when he's being a nuisance.

You should also provide your dog with a variety of interesting chew toys, but don't have them all out all the time. If you see your dog chewing something inappropriate, substitute something better without fussing about it. When your puppy begins to chew the chair leg, offer him another favorite toy, and praise him when he accepts it.

Exercise your dog before you leave the house; a tired dog is less apt to chew. Also, if your dog is not on a regular feeding schedule, his instincts tell him to hunt for food wherever it may be. He may be eating the sofa because he's hungry. If your work prevents you from getting home at the same time every day, consider getting a pet sitter or using a timed self-feeder, a device that allows the animal to eat a little bit at a time all day.

Locking dogs in small, windowless areas is almost bound to result in destructive behavior if your dog is not well crate trained. Dogs should be able to look out the window; they get endless amusement

Consistent training can help desensitize your dog to loud or startling noises.

spying on the neighbors, just as we do. Don't forget to provide toys in the area of confinement.

Noise Phobia

Some dogs seemingly go mad when a thunderstorm arrives. No one is sure why, and answers vary from the ambient electricity, to the drop in barometric pressure, to the noise. Regardless, something about a thunderstorm definitely bothers them!

Many dogs exhibit a perfectly natural terror of almighty nature. Although you will probably never get your thunder-shy GSD to enjoy accompanying you on a death-defying walk during an electrical storm, it is possible to keep him from having fits while safe at home during such an event.

Let's talk about what won't work first:

- **Coddling your dog during a thunderstorm.** That will merely confirm his suspicion that something is terribly, terribly wrong.
- **Punishing your dog.** This will just make him afraid of you.

The following are some solutions that might work:

- **A positive, cheerful attitude.** "Oh, boy, Tucker! A thunderstorm! Isn't that exciting?" Don't carry this too far, though. It would not be a wise idea to actually take your GSD out for a walk in the storm. Thunderstorms are dangerous, and your dog knows this—that's what scares him.
- **Antiphobic drugs.** Some people use tranquilizers or antidepressants in addition to other therapy. Consult with your vet if you are considering antiphobic drugs.
- **Homeopathic and herbal remedies.** If you want to try a more natural route, you can experiment with one of the many products that contain valerian, a sleep-inducing herb. Melatonin, chamomile, St. John's Wort, and hops are also possible candidates. Although these products are available over the counter, you should talk to your vet before giving them to your dog, as some do not react well with other drugs.
- **Pheromones.** You can buy over-the-counter dog-appeasing pheromones that release the same comforting pheromones that

mother dogs release to comfort their puppies. (This remedy may also work with separation anxiety, which is explained later.)

- **A crate.** If your dog is used to being in a crate, it's a very comfortable place for him to be when there's a lot of noise. Putting a cover over the crate will also help assuage his fears.

Fireworks

Fireworks are a source of terror for many dogs. They apparently don't enjoy the sights and sounds of combustibles exploding across the night sky as much as the silent, unobstructed glory of the moon and stars. I can't say that I blame them.

If you want to go see some fireworks, go, but let your GSD stay safe at home. Leave the television on or provide other soothing, familiar sounds, and make sure the house is as secure as possible. Put your dog in his crate and turn off the lights. Dogs feel more comfortable in the dark.

The Fear Factor

It's upsetting to see any dog react fearfully to loud noises or startling situations. Minimize their effects by understanding what to do, which will ensure everyone's safety.

Other Loud Noises

Although fireworks only occur a few times a year and are generally avoidable, the same cannot be said for other loud noises, like vacuum cleaners and other plagues of civilization. You may wish to give up housecleaning altogether on the pretext that vacuuming frightens your dog.

If you feel you must go on cleaning, though, you should attempt to remove your dog from those situations that terrify him or work to desensitize him the same way you would to thunder.

Obsessive-Compulsive Disorders

An obsessive-compulsive disorder (OCD) is a behavior characterized by repetitive and pointless activities like tail chasing or paw licking. These behaviors are usually outgrowths of normal canine behavior, like paw licking instead of grooming, for example. However, in the case of true OCD, the behavior simply does not stop as it would if the dog was simply grooming himself.

In some cases, the precipitating cause of obsessive-compulsive disorder could be an undiagnosed infection. (This seems to be true with some cases of human OCD as well.) Certain diseases, like Cushing's disease, may also bring about the neurological changes that produce OCD. In younger dogs, paw licking or chewing could be a simple nervous habit. Chewing the base of the tail could also

Research has found that dogs who are left alone for a large part of the day suffer more physical health problems than do dogs with adequate companionship.

mean fleas are present. However, if the licking or chewing behavior continues for weeks with no apparent organic cause, especially if carried to the point of raw or bleeding paws, I would suspect OCD arising from misplaced grooming behavior. In many cases, the final result will be a lick granuloma, a scarred or ulcerated area on the inside of one or both legs.

Tail chasing is rather common in herding breeds and may have a genetic component. The spinning dog will ceaselessly spin or chase his tail. Some dogs carry this to the point of bleeding paw pads, and they will often pay almost no attention to any other stimulus. No one knows the exact cause, but it's likely that both genetics and environmental factors play a part.

Solution

Like OCD in human beings, this is not a psychological problem. Although it may have been precipitated by loneliness, illness, or boredom, it cannot be classified as a neurosis. It has an organic component that is best treated medically. It is very seldom cured by getting another dog, mechanical intervention like Elizabethan collars, or by giving your dog something else to do. So-called behavior modification doesn't work very well either.

Mild, early onset cases of OCD can sometimes be contained or cured by conventional behavior therapies, diet, and exercise. Lots of play and perhaps a low-protein, additive-free diet may help. So will a regular schedule (to help relax the dog) in addition to ignoring the behavior if it seems to be primarily an attention-getting device. If you catch the behavior *early* enough, it may be possible to distract your dog by offering play or treats in place of the behavior.

If the neurological changes have already occurred, however, you'll probably need to ask your vet about prescribing an antidepressant. Antidepressants seem to work particularly well if the precipitating cause was an infection, which leaves certain protein markers on cell surfaces. Antidepressants that help control OCD in human beings can also work with dogs. Substantial improvement is seen in two out of three cases.

Running Away and Car Chasing

Running away and car chasing are two problems that you as a responsible dog owner should never have to face. Luckily, these problem behaviors are easily solved!

Solution

To prevent your dog from running away or chasing cars, you should simply keep your dog safely fenced-in outside. This way, he will never have the opportunity to chase cars or run away.

Nowadays, a responsible dog owner simply will not allow her dog to run free. This strategy is so simple I wonder why no one ever thought of it before. Keeping your dog at home protects him from being hit by cars and encountering a variety of other dangers.

Separation Anxiety

Separation anxiety is one of the main reasons people get rid of their dogs. Affected dogs whine, bark, salivate, chew the curtains, eat the couch, or tear up the rug. Some eat holes in the linoleum or devour part of the wall. Some bark without ceasing. Many of these animals are former denizens of the pound or animal shelter; every time they move to a new home, their self-confidence weakens a little more.

According to one estimate, 14 percent of dogs suffer from separation anxiety. Dogs are social beings who were never meant to spend hour after hour away from kith and kin. In fact, they need at least one hour, preferably two, of close human companionship a day to be happy and healthy. Walking, grooming, training, playing, and cuddling all count toward together time. Remember that although your dog may not be the center of your life, you are certainly the center of his. A lonely dog can become stressed, despondent, and destructive. While some dogs seem to manage well enough by themselves, most dogs need companionship— preferably yours. If that is not possible, adding another dog (or even a cat) to the family can soothe anxious moments. Dogs from shelters who have experienced abandonment suffer from separation anxiety the most.

Fortunately, neither you nor your dog has to continue suffering from separation anxiety. Treatment, both medical and behavioral, is available. Drug therapy is a new and very

Your Shepherd cannot run away if he's in a securely fenced yard.

Home Alone

Giving your dog something he will really enjoy chewing just as you leave will make the transition time less stressful. Fill a hard rubber dog chew with peanut butter and give it to him when your coat is on and you're ready to go. Leaving the radio on to a classical music station can help, too.

promising treatment for severe separation anxiety in dogs. However, before medicating your pet, see what behavior modifications you can make to your own lifestyle.

Solution

The following are various ways that you can help alleviate your German Shepherd Dog's separation anxiety:

- **Crate Your Dog.** Crating may help create a sense of security for your dog, and even if it doesn't, he won't be chewing the furniture while he's confined. It's not safe to leave a puppy less than four months of age alone free in the house anyway; he simply does not have the psychological maturity to keep from ripping things into shreds. Don't leave him in the crate for more than four hours at the most, however. He needs both mental and physical stimulation he can't get in a crate. The condition of some dogs may worsen when crated.

- **Desensitize the Dog.** Start desensitizing your dog gradually to being left alone. Of course, you can't take your dog with you to the opera, but it is not unreasonable to expect to be able to leave him alone for a few hours without returning to a war zone. One way you can do this is by getting him used to being on his own, even when you are at home. To accomplish this, discourage him from following you around the house, and give him his own chores to do (like chewing a bone). This doesn't mean you should ignore him; the goal is to build up his confidence and the perception that he's a part of your life, even though you are not paying exclusive attention to him.

Another way you can desensitize your dog to being left alone is to prepare to leave the house without actually doing so. Jiggle the doorknob and jangle your keys. Do this several times a day, and soon your German Shepherd Dog won't necessarily associate you getting out your purse with him being left alone.

When you do leave the house, don't make a big to-do about either departing or returning. Pay no attention to your dog for about 15 minutes or so before you leave. This means you should avoid even looking him, strange as it sounds, because this will actually have a calming effect on him. Looking at him raises his expectations and can make him nervous.

You should only leave your German Shepherd Dog unsupervised for gradually lengthened time periods. Get him used to the idea of you being gone. At first, leave and come back within a minute or two. Give him a toy as you depart, and collect it upon your return. Soon, he'll understand that you'll always return, and he won't become destructive, at least not from separation anxiety. (That doesn't mean he won't get bored, however.) Most people make the mistake of not being gradual enough in their separation training. If your dog behaves well for one hour alone, do not assume he can be safely left for eight hours. Increase his periods alone by only 15 minutes at a time.

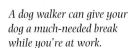

You can leave the radio or television on while you're gone. Studies show that classical music, for example, has a calming effect on dogs. You can also call your dog on the phone and leave him a nice message on the answering machine. Theoretically, the sound of your voice is supposed to have a calming effect on him.

A dog walker can give your dog a much-needed break while you're at work.

- **Don't Overstimulate the Dog.** This means you shouldn't soak him in attention when you're home and then suddenly leave. The contrast will be too much for him to bear. Sometimes, it works better to be rather distant with a dog who is suffering from separation anxiety until he improves. This seems contradictory to the hour or so of attention I suggest giving him, and it may be. A lot depends on the individual dog.

- **Find a Pet Sitter or Dog Walker.** If you must be away from home for an extended period of time, hire someone trustworthy to entertain your dog. This gives him something to look forward to. When you return, you'll find a much quieter, happier dog. This does not have to be an expensive proposition. A responsible neighbor child might be happy to walk your dog for a nominal fee.
- **Get Another Dog or Cat.** Dogs are pack animals. Even though we have

successfully bred them for thousands of years to think of us as their pack, there's no substitute for the real thing. Dogs interact naturally with each other, and just being in the company of their own kind may calm them down. (After all, the other dog won't make him sit or tell him to fetch. They'll just run around and be doggy together.) Your new dog doesn't have to be another German Shepherd Dog; however, it usually works best if both dogs are approximately the same size. If two dogs are too much for you or are forbidden by the landlord, consider getting a cat. Even a cat who steadfastly ignores a dog will draw his attention.

- **Seek Professional Help and/or Medication.** Along with behavior modification, new medications are available. Some people object on principle to medicating their dogs. Although I empathize with those who want to treat their dogs naturally, there are times when modern pharmacology is the best answer. Consult with your veterinarian to see what, if any, medications are right for your German Shepherd Dog.

Shyness

Shyness has a biological basis in both people and animals. We know that in GSDs it can be an inherited trait, and unfortunately, shy GSDs may be prone to fear biting, which is very dangerous. Obviously, environment plays a part in developing or inhibiting shyness, but the key factor is genetic predisposition.

A shy dog who has inherited a shy temperament will always be more timid than the average dog. This does not mean, however, that owners of shy dogs cannot do a great deal to make a timid dog less timid.

Solution

To build a dog's confidence, you must present him with a series of gradually more challenging situations. As long as the program is very gradual, most shyness can be reduced to a manageable level. One way to do this is to socialize your dog through an obedience class. Your main purpose here is socialization, so a puppy kindergarten class is perfect if your dog is the right age. If not, explain the problem to your local kennel club, and they will help you find a suitable class.

Don't rush or force the socialization process. It takes much longer with a shy dog. Also, don't allow strangers to rush up to your dog and begin petting him when you know perfectly well it terrifies him. Let your dog have his personal space where he can breathe safely. As he becomes more confident, the personal space will shrink. Ask strangers to hold out their hands (with a treat) and look away from your dog while offering it. For dogs, eye contact, especially from strangers, is threatening. If your dog absolutely will not take a treat handed to him, have the person place the treat on the ground in front of the dog and then back away.

If you and your dog are faced with a "threatening" situation, don't comfort your dog. Speak cheerfully, and try to distract his attention by playing with him, feeding him, or trotting off together. This isn't the same as running away, although it may feel like it. What you're doing is using his adrenaline in a positive way. The exercise should calm your dog and distract him at the same time. Don't run directly away from the feared thing unless necessary; instead, try going by it at a fast clip.

Shy dogs often work better on a harness than on a collar, and they especially prefer the harness to a choke chain or anything that remotely startles or frightens them. Think like a dog: Would it calm your nerves to be led around on a choke chain, not knowing from one minute to the next when it's going to tighten around your neck? I would take a harness any day!

Although it can be risky with alpha dogs, it's beneficial to play tug-of-war with a shy dog. Let him win; it will help build up his confidence. Owners of retrieving breeds have been doing this for years to build confidence in shy dogs. Play other games, too, particularly ones that enforce the prey drive, like chasing and catching things.

Training your dog is not only fun, but it is necessary as well. A well-trained dog will be a welcome guest, a treasured family member, and your best friend!

Overcoming Shyness

If your dog is overly shy or easily spooked in certain situations, try the following:

- more socialization
- encourage adult strangers to give treats while out in safe situations
- build his confidence
- work with a professional trainer

ADVANCED TRAINING AND ACTIVITIES

With Your German Shepherd Dog

Before taking your dog to the next level beyond basic obedience, it's important to make sure your dog is fit. This is why it's important to have your vet look over your dog to make sure he is ready to begin. She will check your dog for heart, joint, and lung problems first.

Once you get the okay, the next thing to do is build a routine. It's wise to start slowly, usually with a couple of short exercise periods every day. Walking, games like fetch, and even swimming are excellent ways to build your dog's energy and endurance. Heavy panting, stopping, and signs of pain are clues that your dog is not yet ready for a more vigorous workout.

Remember that the German Shepherd Dog is one of the most versatile breeds. If the law allows it, he can do it. In fact, most people have to check their own limitations rather than those of the GSD!

THE CANINE GOOD CITIZEN® PROGRAM

The American Kennel Club's Canine Good Citizen (CGC) Program is a certification program that is designed to reward dogs who have good manners at home and in the community. The two parts of the program stress responsible pet ownership for owners and basic good manners for dogs. All dogs who pass the ten-step test may receive an official, frame-worthy certificate from the American Kennel Club.

The Canine Good Citizen test is open to all dogs, whether mixed breed or purebred, and there is no age limit, although the dog must be old enough to have received his immunizations. You will need a leash and collar (buckle or slip-type collar; no special training collars, such as a prong collar or head halter, are permitted) and a brush or comb for grooming. Your dog should be well groomed and in healthy condition.

This is a great opportunity to educate, bond, and have fun with your dog. You'll both benefit!

CONFORMATION

Conformation showing is a beauty contest. (It's what you see at the Westminster Kennel Club Show every February on television.) For most people, the goal of conformation showing is to win a Championship. To do this, a dog needs to accumulate 15 points at AKC-sanctioned dog shows. Dogs can win as many as five points at a given show, although this is very rare. More commonly, a dog will win one, two, or three points. The number of points your dog can win depends on how many other German Shepherd Dogs were entered in all of the classes.

If you do decide to show your GSD, look at it as a learning experience. If you handle him yourself, you'll gain a lot of knowledge, but if you're a novice, you're probably not giving your GSD his best shot at winning. Experienced handlers know how to make the most of their charge's best points, and they even know which judges are likely to appreciate your dog's finer qualities.

Conformation evaluates dogs based on how well they conform to the written standard of the breed.

There will be several dog shows every weekend during the

spring and summer near you. You can get a feel for how the classes are conducted at these shows. Don't bring your own dog to the show, however, unless he is entered. Most shows have a rule against this practice, because space is limited.

German Shepherd Dog specialties are for this breed only. In the specials class (for champions only), two "special" titles are offered: "Grand Victor" for males and "Grand Victrix" for females. These titles are used only in German Shepherd Dog circles. The judge may also give out a "Select" award for other high-quality dogs.

Choosing a Handler

You can show your own dog for your personal satisfaction and development, or you can enlist the services of a professional handler, who will probably produce better results faster. Choosing the right handler is as important as choosing the right vet or groomer; sometimes a handler who is perfect for one dog just doesn't click with another one. Go to some shows to watch various handlers in and out of the ring; when you find one you like, get her business card and ask around to see what other people have heard of her. If you like what you hear, make an appointment to meet her and discuss your dog's future.

Of course, you may decide to handle your own dog. But before you actually step into the ring, take some handling classes at your local kennel club, and go to a few dog shows. Handling classes can be invaluable. You'll learn dog show protocol, proper terminology, how to dress, and most importantly, you'll learn how to pose and gait your dog.

Conformation in Germany

Germans take their dog shows seriously. Because the GSD was bred to travel as much as 50 miles a day, their show counterparts are put to the test. The shows go on for hours, with the dog working the whole time. (The handlers have to take breaks and switch off, but the dog keeps working.) Also, because the show dogs by necessity have to travel around a ring, the animals' supporters gather about encouraging the animal. They switch off as well, not only because they are exhausted, but because the dog gets bored unless he gets a change of face. This is called "double

"Helpers" in Germany

During the actual class, helpers will shake toys, whistle, talk to the dog, and run alongside in order to call attention to the dog's motion. This is called double handling, forbidden in the United States and the United Kingdom but welcome and almost required at German Shepherd Dog shows in Germany. Space is reserved for them, and they are responsible for making sure the dog has adequate water.

A professional handler can help you achieve better results in a shorter period of time.

Match Shows

If you and your dog are still learning, it's fun to enter a match show. Matches are informal affairs structured very much like a "real show," and you can enter the very day of the event. They are specifically designed for novice handlers and novice dogs, and they are a great way to learn the ropes. You won't receive any points for winning, however, even if your dog turns out to be Best in Match.

handling" in the United States and is technically not permitted, although people do it anyway. Even in the United States, German Shepherd Dogs are paced for a much longer time than are other breeds.

In Germany, a conformation show (Sieger) uses a larger ring that allows for more extended gaiting than is customary in the United States. In these shows, dogs compete for ratings, such as excellent (V) or excellent Select (VA). If more than one dog is judged VA, the best of them will usually be designated VA-1, and he will receive the title "Sieger."

The Canine Good Citizen® Program encourages dogs and their owners to cultivate good manners at home and in the community.

FORMAL OBEDIENCE

Obedience training is the bedrock of all canine sports and companion activities. A willful, disobedient dog cannot achieve success in tracking, conformation, agility, search and rescue, or any of the other myriad activities human do with their dogs unless they are proficient at obedience.

When begun in 1933, AKC obedience trials were designed to foster training and demonstrate a dog's willingness to work closely with people. Today, obedience trials are held at most all-breed dog shows, as well as at many German Shepherd Dog "specialties." Obedience trials were originally created to have several levels, including the long-standing classes of Novice (CD), Open (CDX), and Utility (UD). Later, higher levels of competition were added, like Utility Excellent (UDX) and Obedience Trial Champion (OTCH). The newest title will be awarded to the top dog at the National Obedience Invitational. This dog will become the National Obedience Champion for the entire year.

GSDs do extremely well in obedience trials. Their intelligence and willingness to work consistently places them among the event's winners. And because obedience is a game where every dog can "win," it's a great sport for those who like to show their dogs off but are not keen on formal competitive events. Competitive or not, however, obedience is a highly structured activity with its own special culture. To become proficient in obedience, join your local kennel club and take classes.

To receive a "leg" toward his obedience title, all your dog needs to do is to pass the required events for his level. Currently, there are three levels of Obedience: Novice, Open, and Utility. The Novice and Open levels are further divided into two classes, A and B, with the A classes created for people who have not competed successfully at that level yet, and the B classes for more experienced handlers. Every competition is worth 200 points, and to qualify, your GSD must earn 170 of those points. He has to do this three times under three different judges. If he does, he wins his CD (Companion Dog) title. Higher level competition results in CDX (Companion Dog Excellent) and UD (Utility Dog) titles. Dogs who have earned their UD are eligible to win the coveted OTCH (Obedience Trial Champion), a title earned by outscoring other dogs at several events.

Today, obedience trials are held in conjunction with most all-

The Kennel Club's Good Citizen Dog Scheme

In 1992, the Kennel Club launched a new training program called the Good Citizen Dog Scheme to promote responsible dog ownership in the UK. Since then, over 52,000 dogs have passed the test, which is administered through 1,050 training organizations.

Any dog is eligible to take part in the Good Citizen Dog Scheme, a noncompetitive plan that trains owners and dogs for everyday situations and grants four awards — bronze, silver, gold, and puppy foundation assessment — based on the level of training that both dog and owner have reached together.

For more information, refer to the Kennel Club's website at www.the-kennel-club.org.uk.

Kennel Club Sporting Events

The Kennel Club in the United Kingdom sponsors a variety of events for dogs and their owners to enjoy together. For complete listings, rules, and descriptions, please refer to the Kennel Club's website at www.the-kennel-club.org.uk.

Agility
Introduced in 1978 at Crufts, agility is a fun, fast-paced, and interactive sport. The event mainly consists of multiple obstacles on a timed course that a dog must handle. Different classes have varying levels of difficulty.

Flyball
Flyball is an exciting sport introduced at Crufts in 1990. Competition involves a relay race in which several teams compete against each other and the clock. Equipment includes hurdles, a flyball box, backstop board, and balls.

Obedience
Obedience competitions test owner and dog's ability to work together as a team. There are three types of obedience tests, which include the Limited Obedience Show, Open Obedience Show, and Championship Obedience Show. Competition becomes successively more difficult with each type of show.

Working Trials
The first working trial took place in 1924 and was held by the Associated Sheep, Police, and Army Dog Society. Working trials test a dog's working ability and include five levels of competition known as stakes. Each stake is made up of exercises in control, agility, and nosework.

breed dog shows. To attain the first of these degrees, the CD, a dog must heel on leash, heel free, stand for examination, recall, and complete a long sit (60 seconds) and a long down (3 minutes). When heeling, he'll have to execute left and right turns, stops, and move at various speeds. On the "stand," he'll need to stand still off lead while a judge examines him. The handler must be at least six feet away. The recall requires the dog to sit 30 feet from the handler, come quickly, and then sit. On command, the dog will move to the heel position and sit once more.

Earning a CDX title requires your dog to work entirely off lead. He will have to heel off lead in a figure 8 pattern, drop on recall (going "down" rather than just sitting), retrieve a dumbbell from 20 feet over level ground, retrieve a dumbbell over the high jump, and jump the broad jump. He must also do longer sits (3 minutes) and downs (5 minutes) with the handler completely out of sight.

Utility dogs must follow hand signals for heeling, moving, and standing for examination. The handler cannot use voice signals in this section. Dogs also participate in directed jumping, directed retrieve, and scent discrimination. Dogs can work for their Utility and CDX degrees at the same time.

RALLY OBEDIENCE

Rally obedience became an AKC event as of January 1, 2005. This fast-paced sport is more fun and dog friendly than traditional obedience and offers four title levels for your dog. In rally obedience, you get to talk or even sing to your dog, which is not permitted in regular obedience (except for speaking the command). Unlike in regular obedience, your dog isn't required to have a picture-perfect heel, and there is a lot more variety than in regular obedience. A qualifying score is 70 out of 100 possible points.

TRACKING

Another noncompetitive sport is tracking, which is formally a part of obedience, although the two events are held separately and separate titles are awarded. Your GSD can earn a Tracking Dog title (TD) at a tracking test. German Shepherds absolutely excel at this sport, easily topping all other breeds in titles won. If you have a GSD, this is your event. Go for it!

When tracking, a dog is required to follow a trail by ground scent, not air scent. He will be asked to track an article such as a leather glove that has been dragged through grass and along the ground. He will wear a special "tracking harness," and you will follow your dog on a long lead—in this case the dog is leading you, not the other way around. Three tracking titles are possible: TD (Tracking Dog), TDX (Tracking Dog Excellent), and VST (Variable Surface Tracker).

AGILITY

The GSD's extreme intelligence, athleticism, and willingness to please make him a natural for agility training. Dog agility is modeled on the equestrian version, with dogs jumping obstacles in a stadium-like setting. Your GSD will practice scrambling over A-frames, balancing on a dog walk, crossing the teeter-totter, charging through tunnels, and jumping though hoops. As in obedience, he will compete against other breeds unless the event is held at a GSD specialty.

Obstacles used for agility include the A-frame, dog walk, chute or closed tunnel, pause table, seesaw, weave poles, tire jump, open tunnel, and various kinds of jumps. Handlers may not touch the dogs or the equipment during agility trials.

Agility first made an appearance at the famous UK Crufts Dog Show in 1978, and it is currently the fastest growing dog sport. Dogs don't have to be Mr. Universe to complete well in agility trials. However, the agility dog will need to be able to run full speed for a number of minutes, turn, twist, climb, jump, and dart through tunnels. Many of the obstacles have "contact" zones that require the dog to actually put his feet down in certain places—this prevents dangerous "fly-offs" where the dog could become injured.

In the United States, several organizations hold sanctioned agility events. These include the American Kennel Club, the United States Dog Agility Association (USDAA), and the North American Dog Agility Council, Inc. (NADAC).

Their extreme athleticism and intelligence make German Shepherd Dogs naturals for agility.

SCHUTZHUND TRIALS

In the United States, Germany, and a large part of Europe, Schutzhund is an important element of training in the German Shepherd Dog world. This sport has been developed largely to honor old von Stephanitz, who before he died remarked presciently but sadly, "Take this trouble for me. Make sure my shepherd dog remains a working dog, for I have struggled all my life long for that aim." (In England and Australia, this sport is at the center of controversy, with some people believing it is inappropriate to train dogs to attack as a matter of course.)

Schutzhund events demand the greatest stamina, highest intelligence, and most versatility of all the performance events. The trial covers three phases: tracking, obedience, and protection, usually in a single day. In Germany, dogs must obtain a companion dog (elementary obedience) title first.

In the tracking phase, the dog must follow scent from human

footprints left by a stranger. The tracking can take place on dirt, concrete, grass, or any surface of the judge's choosing. Tracking courses become more difficult at higher Schutzhund levels.

In the obedience phases, the dog works both on- and off-lead. In addition to regular commands, the obedience trial requires dogs to scale walls to retrieve a heavy dumbbell over a jump, an A-frame, and flat ground.

The protection phase includes attack (biting) work in which the dog defends his handler against a staged assault. The "bad guy" wears a special, well-padded sleeve that the dog bites. The dog must cease attack instantly upon command and go into "guard mode," barking furiously at the villain but not actually attacking him.

In the protection stage of a Schutzhund trial, the dog must defend his handler against a staged assault.

Schutzhund trials have three levels of difficulty: Sch I, II, and III. In Germany, a dog must pass through all three levels before he is allowed to compete in the conformation show ring and be bred. In the United States, the closest equivalent is the Working Dog Association North American Sieger Show, held each spring. There is also the United Schutzhund Clubs of America, which started as a sports club but which also holds conformation shows. This organization follows the breed standard as set forth in Germany and by the FCI.

Schutzhund Controversy

In Germany, the US, and most other places, Schutzhund training is critically important, both as a sport and as a "proofing" of character. In the UK, Australia, and one or two other countries, "Schutzhund" was formerly almost a "dirty word," associated with vicious attack dogs and the like. However, there is a British Schutzhund Association (BSA), which is affiliated

If you and your Shepherd love the snow, maybe skijoring is in your future!

with the German Shepherd Dog League of Great Britain (GSDL). The GSDL is a fully functioning member of the World Union of German Shepherd Dog Clubs (WUSV). This was a major move for both groups. The GSDL hopes to learn more about the sport of Schutzhund from the BSA. The organizations will join in helping to establish new training centers throughout the UK where responsible WUSV training programs can be implemented.

FLYBALL

Flyball is a team sport for dogs that was invented in California during the 1970s. It is a relay race that features four dogs per team. The course has four hurdles spaced 10 feet apart and a spring-loaded box that shoots out a tennis ball. The hurdles' height is dependent on the height of the dogs in the team—4 inches below the shoulder height of the shortest dog. Eight inches is the minimum height, and 16 inches is the maximum height. Each dog jumps the hurdles and presses the box to catch the ball and then runs back over the four hurdles. When the dog crosses the starting line, the next dog goes. The first team to have all four dogs run without errors wins the heat.

SKIJORING

Skijoring ("ski-driving") is a traditional Nordic sport that combines cross-country skiing with "carting" (with you as the driver). You simply strap on your skis and attach the dog to yourself with a bungee cord and a 10- to 15-foot tug line. The dog will need a correct pulling harness—not a walking harness or a collar.

Traditionally done with northern breeds like huskies, a well-conditioned GSD more than one and a half years of age is also a superb skiing partner! You need a well-trained dog who will respond instantly to voice commands. Traditional commands are: "Hike!" ("Let's go!"), "Whoa!" ("Stop!"), "Easy" ("Slow down, darn it!"), "Gee!" ("Go right!") and "Haw! ("Go left!" and "On by!"). You should be at least an average cross-country skier before you begin. Do not use metal-edged skis, which could seriously injure your pet!

HERDING

German Shepherds are usually considered to be "sheeptending" dogs, which is not precisely the same thing as "sheepherding" dogs but close enough to be considered in that group. (One of the most frustrating things about putting dogs into "groups" for conformation purposes is that a German Shepherd is equally at home in the Working Group, where he used to be, as well in the Herding Group, where he is now.)

In Germany, training for herding begins when the pup is between four and six months old. The trainer places him in a pen

When herding, the dog's job is to keep the sheep together and ward them away from crops.

with a few very gentle sheep. Soon, the dog learns that sheep instinctively move away from him. His own instinct encourages him to "pressure" the sheep, gathering them into a flock. Then, the dog is taught to patrol the flock, which usually entails keeping the sheep away from the crops or whatever area the farmer designates. If a sheep strays, the dog wards off the sheep from the crop, either by gathering the sheep or by running to the sheep and barking at them, thus frightening them them back to their assigned place. For more serious violations, the dog may grip the sheep's fleece (not flesh), to lead the sheep back. The dogs also learn how to drive the sheep in and out of the fold or barn and how to behave in the barn while sheep are feeding. Early training is done on a long line until the dog learns to work the sheep on his own.

While not many people actually herd sheep anymore, the AKC and American Herding Breeds Association (AHBA) have each developed herding trials, from novice to advanced levels. And don't worry—if you are short on sheep, you can always use ducks. Check out the AKC or AHBA for details on how to get started in this exciting sport!

This pup could grow up to become an excellent dance partner.

MUSICAL FREESTYLE

This sport, otherwise known as dancing with dogs, began in Canada in 1991. In this event, the handler chooses the music and choreographs the movements, so unlike regular obedience, each composition is utterly unique to that team. Typical moves include heeling, spins, jump, weaves, and turns. Dogs are judged on their attention, enthusiasm, and the degree of difficulty involved in the movements. The emphasis is on showcasing the dog's (not the handler's) ability.

You can compete in three separate classes at three different levels. Classes include Individual (one handler, one dog), Brace (two handlers, two dogs), and Team (three or more handlers, each with a dog). A Tandem class (one handler, two dogs) is also offered in the Exhibition Only category. Participants may begin competing with a dog in any class, in either the On-leash or Off-leash Divisions, but must qualify from the Off-leash Division to enter Masters. Titles offered are: MFD (Musical Freestyle Dog), MFX (Musical Freestyle Excellent), and MFM (Musical Freestyle Master). This is not currently an AKC event.

SERVICE DOGS

Seeing Eye Inc. was founded in 1929, and it is probably the most famous of service dog programs, though Guiding Eyes for the Blind and Canine Companions for Independence are others. German Shepherd Dogs have been used by these organizations for many years to assist the visually impaired.

Today, German Shepherds are used for much more than leading the blind, although they still excel at this as well. They also work to help people with orthopedic difficulties, as hearing dogs, and in many other capacities. The service dog leads a privileged life in many ways (after all, he gets to be with his owner 24 hours a day and is allowed to go anywhere), but few dogs of any breed are up to the task. They must be highly responsive and trainable, in perfect health, and of a faultless temperament. Most dogs "fail" service school within their first month.

Service dogs must possess a variety of attributes, including confidence, intelligence, and fearlessness.

Service dogs who do make the grade should have the following qualities:

- Confidence, curiosity, and extroversion
- Intelligence
- Fearlessness
- Adaptability to different climates
- Good sense of smell
- Strength and speed
- Good socialization and tolerance of humans
- Perseverance
- Ability to be muzzled
- Ability to attack and release on command (attack dogs)

Patrol dogs must pass a "prey test" that evaluates their ability to chase down, grasp, and carry a moving object. They are also taught to ride quietly, to search for a suspect in a building, and

to attack immediately if the handler is attacked. He must not react to gunfire.

Sadly for lovers of German Shepherd Dogs, fewer of them now work as police dogs than was formerly the case. One reason is the increased popularity of the breed, which has led many breeders to breed for show and pet rather than as a general working dog. Many fanciers believe that conformation breeders do not work hard enough to eliminate undesirable characteristics from the gene pool. Even in the present day German korung (breed evaluation), many people believe

Patrol dogs are taught to ride quietly, as well as search for suspects in buildings and attack if their handler is attacked.

that insufficient attention is given to prey drive and fighting instinct. Others complain that dogs are evaluated merely on Schutzhund scores rather than on total working ability.

Military and Federal Agency Dogs

The United States military uses dogs, mostly German Shepherd Dogs, Dutch Shepherds, and Belgian Malinois, to scout, search buildings, detect explosives, and attack on command. Currently, about 1,800 dogs are in service. Oddly, American military dogs come exclusively from Europe and are procured by the 341st Squadron, based at Lackland Air Force Base in Texas. The squadron is also responsible for obtaining all dogs for the Department of Defense, the Secret Service, the Federal Aviation Administration, and other federal agencies. These dogs work search and rescue missions, accompany police on patrol, detect bombs and drugs, hunt down criminals, and help investigate arson.

While German Shepherd Dogs the world over have earned their stripes as genuine canine heroes, the law has been slow to recognize their accomplishments. According to the 1979 Federal Property and Administrative Services Act, military dogs were considered as "equipment" to be discarded (killed) when they retired from duty. In 1997, that law was amended to let handlers adopt the dogs when they became too old for work. Unfortunately, the amended law left out many dogs who could not be adopted by their handlers. Some of these old animals were simply used to "train" new recruits and kept in cages until the army got around to killing them. New legislation, backed by the Humane Society of the United States, the ASPCA, the Doris Day Animal League, and the American Veterinary Medical Association, now permits these dogs to go to adopted homes.

SEARCH AND RESCUE

Search and rescue handlers are volunteers who must be physically fit, love working outside, have sufficient time, and enjoy working with their dogs. Necessary equipment includes working harnesses, long lines, vests for the dogs, radios, flashlights, hard hats, compasses, and packs to carry items on the trail. (Don't assume you will be given these things!) Handlers should also become certified in cardiopulmonary resuscitation and first aid.

Some search dogs are trackers who follow a human scent laid down along the ground. Bloodhounds are most famous at this for their ability to follow an extremely old scent and their legendary ability to concentrate on just one thing at a time. German Shepherd Dogs, however, are frequently used for their versatility and ease of training. The GSD nose can match that of a Bloodhound if the scent is reasonably fresh. (The ability to follow a very old scent is counterproductive in the wild—wolves wouldn't catch any dinner

German Shepherd Dogs excel at search and rescue, and their nose can match that of a Bloodhound if the scent is fairly fresh.

Walking or jogging with your German Shepherd Dog is a great way to bond with him and exercise him at the same time.

by trailing around after 100-hour-old scents.)

Some search dogs are trained to find missing persons by following an airborne scent. This is the most efficient method of searching large areas quickly. It does not require clothing or other items belonging to the missing person. It is calculated that a dog is equivalent to about 20 searchers in good conditions and many more in poor conditions. Dogs work equally well in the dark and use their senses of smell and hearing to the fullest under these conditions.

In ideal conditions, a dog can pick up a human scent from about 500 meters. Dog teams can be deployed by helicopter to remote areas where they can quickly begin to start searching. Search and rescue dogs work on lead but learn to alert their handlers to a find.

EXERCISE, GAMES, AND ACTIVITIES

Maybe you're not interested in organized events. That's fine, because you and your GSD can have a great time just by yourselves!

Walking and Jogging

Walking or jogging is a great way to bond with your dog in a healthful, low-stress event that you'll both like. It has been shown that people who have a dog buddy for a walking partner do better than those people who do it alone—and your dog will enjoy it as well!

If you decide to walk or jog with your German Shepherd Dog, begin slowly. Work up to a half hour or so of vigorous activity several times a week.

Frisbee®

This popular sport can be physically stressful for canine athletes. Dogs were not meant to jump and twist, as these actions are hard on the spine. To play safely, it's important to know the physical capabilities of your dog. Young dogs in particular are at risk, so if your dog plays, don't overtax him.

Tug-of-War

For a long time, people were told not to play tug with their dogs, as it made them aggressive and dominant. This is not true, although you probably should avoid this game with an animal who has had dominance or aggression problems in the past. For the normal GSD, however, tug-of-war is a perfectly suitable game. It provides great exercise and can be played in a small area.

Select a simple tug toy like a tug rope that the dog will come to recognize as the cue for the game, and use it only for tug-of-war. Devise a special command to begin the game, like "let's tug!" Your dog will naturally want to grab the tug rope. If he grabs the rope without permission, don't play—he should release it on command. If he does not do this, teach him by trading the rope for a treat. As soon as you get the rope from him, give it right back and praise him. This will make him more amenable to giving up his cherished rope. If he runs off with the toy, don't chase him. He'll soon return with it for more tugs.

You can also interrupt the game with a few obedience commands from time to time. This will sharpen his skills and keep him listening to you. Don't allow the dog to touch you with his teeth. If you receive a nip, stop the game immediately for at least five minutes. He'll get the picture.

Your German Shepherd Dog is your lifetime companion, so his activities should not be restricted to sitting on the couch watching you eat. In fact, these multi-talented dogs excel at a variety of endeavors, and there are almost no limits to the kinds of sports and activities that the two of you can enjoy together.

Detection Dogs

Arson dogs are trained to locate and detect different substances used to start fires, including gasoline, kerosene, odorless lamp oil, lacquer thinner, and lighter fluid. These dogs can detect less than a drop of these liquids at an arson site.

HEALTH
of Your German Shepherd Dog

Nothing is more important than your German Shepherd Dog's good health. Luckily, this is one area in which you have a lot of control! On the other hand, it sometimes takes a sharp and observant owner to discern when his or her dog may be suffering pain. German Shepherd Dogs are stoic animals who will work and play through a lot of pain. This is because in the old days, there was no advantage in letting your rival know when you felt out of sorts—he might eat you! Today, there is no reason for your German Shepherd Dog to suffer needlessly from pain or illness. You are responsible for helping to keep him in great condition by feeding him a top-quality diet, grooming him regularly, brushing his teeth, and giving him plenty of attention and exercise. Performing a weekly home health check will also help you spot many of the most common problems before they become serious.

TAKING YOUR DOG TO THE VET

Other than you, your veterinarian is your dog's best friend. In order for her to do the best possible job, it's your responsibility to make sure your dog receives regular physical examinations, including a "baseline" so that you can get "normal" values. It also helps if you find a vet who is familiar with the German Shepherd Dog. Call your local German Shepherd Dog club to find out what vet the members use.

A routine exam will include a check of your dog's eyes, ears, mouth, heart, and lungs. Your vet will feel around for lumps, manipulate his hips, and so on. If you take your dog to the vet while he's healthy for a routine checkup, he'll have a pleasant experience and won't associate the vet with pain.

VACCINATIONS

Vaccines are lifesavers and a definite must for puppies. They have also recently become one of the most controversial elements of veterinary medicine. How much, how often, and what diseases should be covered are the subjects of ongoing discussion. However, different veterinarians have different protocols for the spacing of these injections. Have a talk with your veterinarian about her

In the US, every dog needs a rabies shot, but this won't be given until he is about four months old. Getting a rabies vaccination for your dog is not only safe and sensible, it is mandatory everywhere in the United States. Puppies should be immunized against this disease between 12 and 24 weeks of age.

A routine physical examination is essential to maintaining your GSD's health.

own vaccination protocol, and don't be afraid to ask questions.

A vaccine works by priming an animal's immune response against a specific disease. The vaccine stimulates the immune system with a nonpathogenic virus or bacteria, one that has been killed or modified in such a way that it no longer poses a danger to the pet. The dog then develops "memory cells" that help him fight off the dangerous pathogenic form of the virus when it is later encountered.

In order to obtain the best response from a vaccine, puppies and unvaccinated older dogs are given repeated doses. Puppies receive multiple vaccines every two to four weeks to stimulate the immune system to achieve a long-term response at the time that the mother's antibodies disappear. As long as the maternal antibodies are present, the pup will have some protection against diseases, but he will not receive long-term protection from a vaccination. Although it is commonly believed that a certain number of vaccinations must be given, the number of injections has nothing to do with immunity. Protection is achieved by giving a vaccine at a time when maternal antibodies won't interfere. (This doesn't apply to rabies vaccines, however. Rabies vaccines are in a somewhat different category, as they are given with killed vaccines, rather than a modified live vaccine.)

Newborn puppies cannot be vaccinated because they have inherited some protection in the form of antibodies from their mothers that will block the commercial vaccine. Only when the maternal antibodies drop will a commercial vaccine become effective. Unfortunately, there is a dangerous window when the maternal antibodies are too low to protect the puppy but still high enough to block the commercial vaccine. At this time, the puppy is most at risk

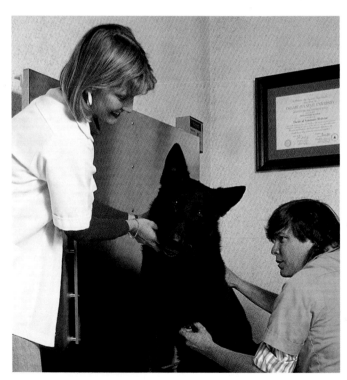

Neutering (Spaying and Castrating)

Unless you own a show dog, please consider spaying or castrating your German Shepherd Dog. Spaying a female dog refers to the removal of the ovaries and uterus, while castration refers to the removal of a male dog's testicles. Neutering has numerous health benefits, such as eliminating or reducing the risk of various cancers of the reproductive system, including prostate cancer in males and mammary cancer in females. It also eliminates the possibility of uterine infections in females. Additionally, neutering your pet will help ease the problem of dog overpopulation. Right now, there are not enough good homes for all of the dogs who are born every day. Even if you could find homes for all of your dog's puppies, what about their puppies? At one time, it was believed that dogs could not be safely neutered before the age of six months; however, modern advances in surgery have made early neutering possible.

for many viral diseases. The length and timing of this window is variable from litter to litter and even from puppy to puppy.

Vaccination Protocol

In general, six to nine weeks is the earliest and safest time to inaugurate a commercial vaccination program, although some veterinarians recommend administering a parvovirus vaccine at five weeks of age. Vaccinating puppies any younger than this, especially with modified live vaccines, can lead to problems. Remember, vaccines do not work immediately; a minimum of five days must pass before you can say that your dog is safely vaccinated.

The AVMA Council on Biologic and Therapeutic Agents' Report on Cat and Dog Vaccines has recommended that the core (essential) vaccines for dogs include distemper, canine adenovirus-2 (hepatitis and respiratory disease), and canine parvovirus-2.

Noncore vaccines include leptospirosis, coronavirus, canine parainfluenza and *Bordetella bronchiseptica* (both factors in "kennel cough"), and *Borrelia burgdorferi* (Lyme disease). Talk to your vet about what is necessary in your area.

The following is a possible vaccination schedule for the average puppy. However, your dog is an individual, so it's important to check with your vet to see what is best for him.

Diseases to Protect Against

Although vaccination protocols differ from place to place and even from vet to vet, consider vaccinating your German Shepherd Dog puppy against the following diseases.

A killed vaccine uses dead viruses to protect against disease. Modified live vaccines use living viruses that have been modified so that they cannot reproduce.

Puppy Vaccination Schedule

Age	Vaccination
5 weeks	**Parvovirus:** for puppies at high risk of exposure to parvo, some veterinarians recommend vaccinating at 5 weeks.
6-9 weeks	**Coronavirus:** where coronavirus is prevalent. Combination vaccine without leptospirosis.
12 weeks or older	**Rabies:** Given by your local veterinarian (age at vaccination may vary according to local law).
12-15 weeks	Combination vaccine **Leptospirosis:** include leptospirosis in the combination vaccine where leptospirosis is a concern, or if traveling to an area where it occurs. **Coronavirus:** where coronavirus is a concern. **Lyme:** where Lyme disease is prevalent or if you're going somewhere it is prevalent.
Adult (boosters)	Combination vaccine **Leptospirosis:** include leptospirosis in the combo vaccine where leptospirosis is a problem if you're going somewhere it is prevalent. **Coronavirus:** where coronavirus is a concern. **Lyme:** where Lyme disease is a problem or if you're going somewhere it is prevalent. **Rabies:** Given by your local veterinarian (stipulated interval between vaccinations varies according to state or local law, usually one to three years).

Most vets now give booster shots only every three years. Annual vaccinations are no longer considered necessary.

Parvovirus

Parvovirus is a highly contagious, deadly virus that first appeared in 1978. It attacks the white blood cells, intestinal tract, and even the heart muscles. Symptoms include depression, appetite loss, vomiting, diarrhea, and bleeding. Most dogs who contract this disease die, even with excellent veterinary care. To make matters worse, parvo is a cold-hardy virus, which means it can survive in infected feces at temperatures as low as 20°F. The incubation period is from two to seven days.

Distemper

Distemper is the main killer of dogs worldwide. It destroys the nervous system and attacks every tissue in the body. It is caused by an airborne, measles-like virus. The incubation period is from 7 to 21 days, and initial symptoms include lethargy, fever, runny nose, and yellow discharge from the eyes. Vomiting and diarrhea are also seen in almost all dogs. The dog will show labored breathing and lose his appetite. Later symptoms include a nervous twitch and thickening of the paw pads and nose pad, which is why the disease was once known as "hardpad." Dogs who progress to this stage are unlikely to make a complete recovery.

Hepatitis

Hepatitis, a serious disease caused by an adenovirus, is most dangerous in puppies. It is spread by contact with an infected dog or with his urine or feces. The white blood cell count drops, and some dogs experience blood-clotting problems. It also affects the kidneys and liver. Symptoms include high fever, red mucous membranes, depression, and loss of appetite. Small blood spots may appear on the gums, and the eyes may appear bluish. Dogs who recover often experience chronic illnesses, and they may shed the virus for months, infecting others. Luckily, this disease is seldom seen nowadays, largely because of effective vaccines.

A vaccine works by priming the dog's immune response against a specific disease.

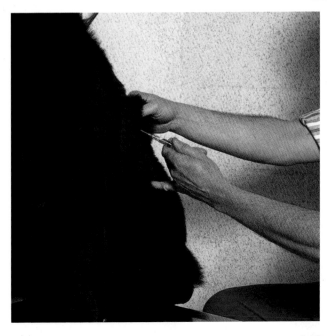

Leptospirosis

Leptospirosis is a bacterial infection that can be passed on to human beings. Dogs can contract this disease through exposure to the urine of an infected dog, rat, or wildlife. Lepto affects the liver and kidneys, and in its most dangerous form, can even shut the kidneys down. Treatment includes antibiotics and in cases of kidney failure, dialysis. A vaccine is available for some forms of leptospirosis; however, many vets do not recommend its use, especially for young puppies. (Because leptospirosis is a bacterial infection, the vaccinations are short lived and can cause adverse reactions. Also, the disease is a problem only in a few places.) The "older" forms of lepto are seldom seen nowadays, and the vaccine can cause reactions in some dogs. Recently, the disease has returned in a new and virulent strain, one that was previously seen only in horses and cows. A vaccine against this lepto strain is currently being tested.

Bordetellosis (Kennel Cough)

Many organisms can cause this condition, which is like a bad cold in older dogs but more serious in puppies. True to its name, dogs infected with bordetella cough, wheeze, hack, and sneeze. It can spread very rapidly through a kennel. The vaccine commonly given for kennel cough, however, does not protect against all forms of the disease. No cure exists—only supportive treatment, and in some cases, antibiotics.

Bordetella can spread very rapidly through a kennel, causing dogs to cough, wheeze, hack, and sneeze.

Coronavirus

Coronavirus is a disease related to the human cold that can cause gastrointestinal disease. Coronavirus is passed through food that has been contaminated by the feces of an infected dog. It is very contagious and causes vomiting, diarrhea, and depression, symptoms similar to those of parvovirus. Fortunately, it is not quite as severe as parvovirus. The stool of the dog will also be yellowish. This disease is most serious in puppies, and there is no real treatment—only supportive care. The vaccine is only recommended in areas where coronavirus is rampant.

Lyme Disease

Lyme disease is carried primarily by the deer tick and was first identified in Old Lyme,

Connecticut, during the 1970s. It is now endemic in most of the United States, especially in the northeast. The incubation period is from two to five months. It causes acute, intermittent lameness and fever, as well as heart and kidney disease. If untreated, your dog can develop permanent arthritis and other forms of degenerative joint disease. It is advisable to give your dog this vaccine if you live in an endemic area and your dog spends a lot of time traipsing in the woods.

Adverse Reactions

In rare cases, your dog might react negatively to a vaccine. Reactions vary with the type of vaccine used and the age of the vaccinated animal. However, compared with the risks of *not* vaccinating, the associated risks are tiny.

The most severe and rarest (1 in every 15,000 vaccinations) reaction to a vaccination is called anaphylaxis, a life-threatening, immediate allergic reaction to something injected. Anaphylactic reactions are more commonly associated with the use of killed vaccines like rabies, canine coronavirus, and leptospirosis. That's because killed vaccines have more viral or bacterial particles per dose and also have added chemicals to boost the dog's immune response. These same features increase the risk of an allergic response.

If untreated, anaphylaxis results in shock and respiratory and cardiac failure. This reaction usually occurs within minutes to less than 24 hours of the vaccination. If you think your dog is having an anaphylactic reaction, get emergency veterinary care for him right away. Epinephrine should be given *as soon as possible*. Your vet may also want to administer intravenous fluids, oxygen, and other medications.

PARASITES

Parasites make their living off your dog, and most of them make your dog sick in the process. However, there's no need for this! Nearly all diseases resulting from parasite infestation are completely preventable.

Parasites cause problems that can result in something as simple as mild itching or something much more severe, such as death. External parasites include mites (sarcoptic, demodex, ear, and cheyletiella), fleas, and ticks. Internal parasites usually include worms like roundworm, hookworm, whipworm, tapeworm, and

Rethinking Vaccine Protocol

Dogs at low risk of disease exposure may not need annual boosters for most diseases. Consult with your local veterinarian to determine the appropriate vaccination schedule for your dog. A combination vaccine, often called a 5-way vaccine, usually includes adenovirus cough and hepatitis, distemper, parainfluenza, and parvovirus. Some combination vaccines may also include leptospirosis (7-way vaccines) and/or coronavirus. The inclusion of either canine adenovirus-1 or adenovirus-2 in a vaccine will protect against both adenovirus cough and hepatitis; adenovirus-2 is preferred. Combination vaccines are very convenient, but there are problems with them. For example, immunity to canine distemper is long (several years), but for leptospirosis, it is relatively short (several months). Putting them on the same schedule, then, may not make sense.

heartworm. Many of these parasites can be prevented or kept under control with preventive medications.

External Parasites

External parasites live on but not inside your dog's body. With the exception of some species of mites, they are usually visible.

Fleas

Over 2,200 species of flea exist worldwide, but fortunately, most of them live elsewhere than on your dog. In fact, there is no reason for the contemporary dog to become afflicted with fleas. It still happens, though, and the ingestion of even one flea containing a tapeworm larva is enough to transmit tapeworm. It can even cause an allergic dog to develop itchy flea dermatitis, which is caused by certain enzymes in flea saliva.

The most common flea to attack dogs is the cat flea (*Ctenocephalides felis*). The cat flea can lay 50 eggs a day for 100 days. These smooth, tiny eggs usually fall onto the carpet or into the couch. A few days later, they hatch into larvae. The larvae live largely on flea feces. About a week later, the larvae spin themselves tiny cocoons and snooze away for a variable period of time, usually a couple of weeks but occasionally several months. When they wake up, they're hungry, and your dog is on the menu!

One of the most important things to remember when dealing with fleas is this: Don't wait for your pet to start scratching! Even if

One great reason to live in high altitudes is that these places are almost flea-free. Fleas can't stand the high altitude!

you use a good flea preventive, it doesn't hurt to check your dog for fleas every time you groom him. Glide your thumbs against the growth pattern of the fur, or use a flea comb. The groin, base of the tail, and neck are popular flea hangouts. Even if you don't see any actual fleas, the black deposits they leave will provide a clue to their presence.

In the old days, people tried to control fleas with topical sprays, powders, dips, collars, and yard sprays. While some people still resort to these old-fashioned methods, most up-to-date owners choose to control fleas with a capsule, or they use a spot-on liquid applied to the skin between the shoulder blades. Some products are available from your veterinarian, although you can get others (although they are somewhat shorter lived and less effective) at the pet supply or grocery store. Some people have also had luck with natural alternatives to conventional flea or tick medications. Garlic, for example, has been popular for centuries. Not all natural alternatives are equally effective, however. It's important to consult with your veterinarian before selecting a particular remedy.

Ticks

Ticks carry Lyme disease, Rocky Mountain spotted fever, ehrlichiosis, haemobartonellosis, babesiosis, tick paralysis, hepatozoonosis, and a host of other diseases. They don't annoy a dog on the surface as much as fleas do, because they don't scamper

Inspect your dog for parasites like fleas and ticks after he's been playing outdoors.

Roundworms are usually harmless in adult dogs, but they can be dangerous when passed to puppies through their mothers.

around or deposit feces everywhere. However, these are also the reasons why they're easy for humans to overlook.

Ticks have four life stages:

- Egg
- Six-legged larva
- Eight-legged nymph
- Adult

Dogs most frequently meet up with ticks when they wander into woodlands and brush. Ticks have a special sensory device (called "Haller's organ") that allows them to sense humidity, odors, heat, movement, and presence of a host. Ticks climb up to the tips of grass or the edge of a twig and wait for an animal or human victim to pass by. At that point, they drop off the twig or blade of grass and attach themselves, burrowing close to the skin. Then, they actually insert their heads beneath the skin to gorge on blood.

If a tick attacks your German Shepherd, pull it off with a pair of fine-tipped tweezers. Wear gloves if possible. Don't bother trying to smother the tick with petroleum jelly or burning it. Grip it as close to the head as possible. (You want to avoid crushing the tick and forcing its bacteria-laden contents into your German Shepherd.)

Once the tick is out, throw it in some alcohol to kill it, or flush it down the toilet. While ticks may not die if flushed down the toilet, they're not going anywhere, either. Clean the area of the bite with a disinfectant and wash your own hands. The bite wound may develop into a welt from the tick's saliva, but this doesn't mean the tick's head is stuck in there. Give it some time; it should heal in about a week. If you believe that an infection or abscess is forming, however, take your dog to the vet.

Lice

Lice are not particularly common in dogs, but if your German Shepherd Dog does become infested, intense itching and irritation may occur. These chewing creatures spend their entire life cycles on the dog—from the egg stage to the adult stage—and live for about a month. As the dog scratches, he can open the way to bacterial, viral, or fungal infections.

Lice can be discouraged with ordinary flea products. By the way, the human head louse or crab louse can also infect a dog if it can't find anything better.

Mites

These arachnids appear in various species, several of which are troublesome to dogs.

- **Demodex canis (mange mite)**: Mange mites are nearly always present somewhere on a dog (you have them, too—in your eyelashes and on your eyebrows), but they don't usually cause trouble, since the immune system keeps them well under control. Sometimes, however, the immune system doesn't do its job well. In that case, the mites multiply and crowd the hair follicles, causing them to fall out. The result is hair loss and itchy, swollen, red skin.
  A localized form of mange may appear on puppies who have an immature immune system, but it will probably resolve itself without treatment. A more serious, generalized form usually shows up on older dogs who also have a compromised immune system. This form requires intensive therapy involving dips in mite

and tick killer. A complete cure may take up to six months. Generalized demodex is often a sign that the dog has another problem, like an autoimmune condition or a serious underlying disease, like cancer.

- **Sarcoptes scabiei (sarcoptic mange)**: Sarcoptic mange is caused by the scabies mite, also known as the "itch mite." Both humans and dogs can get sarcoptic mange. People can contract a temporary case from their pets that lasts about six days, although these mites do not actually reproduce on humans. Puppies and young children are more likely to be affected than adults of either species.

In dogs who are affected by the scabies mite, the female burrows into the skin and lays her eggs. When they hatch into larvae, the larvae dig around and form nasty lesions, causing secondary infections. Affected dogs develop matted hair and a yellowish crust on their skin. This mange is treated with special shampoos, pills, or injections. A good insecticide needs to be applied to the entire area (including bedding) where the dog lives to prevent reinfection.

- **Cheyletiella yasguri (walking dandruff)**: This mite's charming name is indicative of its uncharming habit of producing crud and hair loss on your dog. Fortunately, it doesn't cause the severe itchiness of the other mites and doesn't cause any really serious health problems. Your vet can easily treat it with a special pesticide.

- **Otodectes cynotis (ear mites)**: The ear mite infests both the external ear and the ear canal, nibbling away at the loose skin there. Dogs with ear mites shake their heads and dig at their ears. There will be a nasty discharge or even a hematoma or swelling in the ear from self-mutilation.

  To treat ear mites, the ear needs to be thoroughly cleaned and then treated with a good commercial ear mite killer. Over-the-counter treatments are available. However, because there are many causes of itchy ears that require different treatment protocols (and because home treatment can complicate the diagnosis for the vet), dogs with ear problems should be examined by a vet prior to treatment.

Ehrlichiosis

Ehrlichiosis is a parasitical infection of the white blood cells. This disease is caused by the rickettsial organism *Ehrlichia canis*; the most common vector is the brown dog tick. Ehrlichia infection can cause a number of clinical signs, including lethargy, weight loss, anemia, and loss of appetite. Some dogs have hemorrhages under the skin or around the gums, swollen lymph nodes, soreness, nasal discharges, spinal pain, blood in the urine, and eye problems. A chronic infection can also occur if the acute infection is not treated. The disease is diagnosed by testing serum using an immunofluorescent antibody test, which indicates exposure. In the presence of clinical signs or if the antibody titer rises after treatment or stays consistently high, infection is strongly suspected.

Ehrlichia is normally susceptible to treatment with tetracycline antibiotics, including doxycycline. The chances of survival are good if the disease is recognized early and treated aggressively.

Internal Parasites

Parasites are so clever that they hide inside your dog where you can't see them. Just because you can't see them doesn't mean they can't do any harm, though. The danger with parasites is that they can do quite a lot of damage before you notice they are even present at all. This is an important reason to keep your dog on parasite preventive all year round.

Internal parasites can cause problems such as diarrhea, weight loss, anemia, and vomiting. In some cases, there are no signs, and the worms can be passed from mothers to offspring during pregnancy. The following are some common worms.

Tapeworm

Dogs can acquire tapeworms from eating infected fleas (or more rarely, lice). A tapeworm infestation doesn't have many signs, and you probably won't even know your pet is affected unless you notice the rice-like segments of the worms in your dog's feces or near his anus. Your vet can prescribe a special dewormer to rid your dog of them.

Another common species, *Taenia pisiformis*, can be picked up by ingesting infected rabbits and rodents.

Roundworm

Roundworms, or ascarids, are the most common internal parasites. They're usually harmless in adult dogs but can be dangerous when they are passed to puppies through their mothers. Nearly all puppies are born with roundworms, and severely affected puppies can die from them. German Shepherd Dogs as young as two weeks can start deworming treatment, which is continued every couple of weeks until the eggs are no longer found in the stool sample. Infected puppies typically vomit and have a rough coat, bad breath, diarrhea, and a potbelly. They are usually infected through the placenta before birth and from the mother's milk afterward. (This is true even if the mother has been dewormed.)

Several commercial preparations are available to treat roundworms.

Whipworm

Whipworms live in the large intestine and cecum (a pouch at the beginning of the large intestine). The whipworms, which grow to 3 inches long, actually stab through the intestine, feeding on blood and fluids. A severe infection can cause anemia, pain, and weight loss. Some dogs will also develop periodic, smelly diarrhea.

Whipworms do not attack humans, but that's the only good thing I can say about them. They are hard to get rid of, too. Each female whipworm may produce eggs that are shed in the dog's stool. These eggs may survive in the soil for up to five years waiting to infect a passing dog. There is no effective method for killing whipworm eggs in the soil. The eggs are resistant to most cleaning methods, and reinfection is likely. To prevent exposure, any feces in the yard should be picked up on a daily basis. Consult with your veterinarian for treatment and control of whipworm.

Parasite Control

The Companion Animal Parasite Council, a group of veterinarians and other healthcare providers recommends year-round parasite control. Many parasites, including roundworms, hookworms, and whipworms, are present all year in virtually all regions of the United States. Only about half of pet owners who treat for parasitic infection during the summer continue to do so during the winter.

Hookworm

Hookworms get their name from the hook-like "teeth" they use to attach to the intestinal wall. Hookworms are found mostly in warmer climates. They are very small (usually about 1/8 of an inch), but they can extract enormous amounts of blood from your dog, causing intestinal distress, bloody diarrhea, and in severe cases, anemia. Dogs can become infected with hookworm orally, through the skin, through the mother dog's placenta, and through the mother's milk. It has been reported that one adult female hookworm can produce as many as 20,000 eggs a day!

Your vet can detect hookworms easily though a microscopic examination of a stool sample. Adults can be killed with several medications given orally or injected. Usually, the dog will require another treatment within two to four weeks. Most heartworm prevention products contain a drug that will prevent hookworm infections. However, these products will not kill adult hookworms, so dogs must be treated for adult hookworms first. The environment may also be treated, and some are even safe to use on grass.

Ringworm

Despite the name, ringworm is a transmissible fungal infection usually characterized by circular hair loss and scaly skin. It is not usually itchy. Most cases disappear by themselves, but more severe cases can be treated with antifungal medications.

If your dog gets ringworm, have him (and all the other dogs and cats in your home) treated, and then clean your house thoroughly. This includes getting the air filters changed and disinfecting animal bedding, brushes, and combs with bleach. Ringworm spores can float around in the air for years.

Giardia

Giardia is a common protozoan parasite that can infect any mammal, including humans. (In fact, it is possible for dog owners to contract it from their pets.) Giardia has two life stages: the cyst and the trophozoite. Dogs can become infected if they drink cyst-contaminated water, lick cyst-contaminated feces, or devour cyst-infected prey. When the giardia enter the dog's gastrointestinal system, they enter a new phase of life and reproduce rapidly.

Dogs can become infected with giardia by drinking cyst-contaminated water.

The main signs of giardiasis are vomiting and diarrhea. Infected humans report cramping and nausea also, but these symptoms are difficult to detect in dogs. If the condition is not treated, infected animals can suffer weight loss and continued periods of vomiting and diarrhea. A stool sample is sometimes used for diagnosis, although even that can be hit or miss. A blood test known as the ELISA blood test is more accurate, because it looks for a specific protein particular to giardia. This test is quite a bit more expensive than the fecal test, however. Several drugs are available to treat giardiasis, and there is also a vaccine available. Discuss these options with your vet.

To protect your pet from contracting giardiasis in the first place, keep your yard picked up and prevent your dog from drinking contaminated water sources. This is tougher than it sounds; even pristine mountain streams and tap water can contain the organism.

Heartworm

The heartworm is a long, slender worm that passes from mosquitoes to your dog in the larval stage. The larvae enter the bloodstream and wind up in the heart, where they continue to develop into adult worms. The adults produce larvae that circulate in the blood. Their life cycle is pretty complicated, because these new larvae can't grow into adults until they are ingested by a second mosquito, where they molt and are redeposited into another (or even the same) dog. The blood contains microscopic heartworm babies. Once inside the dog, the baby heartworms can grow into truly hideous adults over a foot long. The disease causes serious irreversible damage to the heart, the lungs, and the arteries feeding them.

Adult hookworms do not infect humans; however, the larvae can burrow into human skin. This causes itching, commonly called ground itch, but the worms do not mature into adults.

Heartworm is present throughout most of the United States, especially in areas with warmer climates. Over 244,000 dogs test positive for infection each year. The only way to tell if your dog has heartworm is for him to be checked by a vet. She can perform a simple blood test for heartworm, which will detect the presence of the worm before any symptoms appear. If the disease is more advanced, your dog may cough, lose weight, or experience heart failure.

The treatment for heartworm is arduous for the dog and expensive for you; however, it's great to know that the disease is easily prevented. Heartworm prevention is safer and easier than treatment, and it should be started by the time your dog is 12 weeks old. Many kinds of heartworm preventions also protect against intestinal parasites or even fleas. Check with your vet to see what plan is right for your dog. A once-a-month prescription tablet or topical treatment will do the trick. Discuss your options with your veterinarian. Regardless of which preventative you choose, however, it's important that the dog be tested for heartworm first. The medication causes the death of any heartworms in the body, and if a dog is heartworm positive, the sudden death of the worms could clog his arteries and kill him.

COMMON DISORDERS AND DISEASES

One of the few downsides to owning a German Shepherd Dog is the fact that they are prone to many diseases, more so than many other breeds. This is partly because of their popularity. Popular breeds tend to have more health problems than less popular ones, in part due to indiscriminate breeding practices.

Beyond the Symptoms

More than one-third of dogs living in the United States and Europe may be infected with gastrointestinal parasites. Many, however, are asymptomatic, meaning that they do not exhibit any symptoms.

Allergies

An allergy is nothing more than an oversensitive or inappropriate physiological response to a substance (referred to as an allergen). Allergies are common in many breeds of dogs, including German Shepherd Dogs.

Allergic Dermatitis (AD)

This is a general term that describes a complex of skin allergies. The body recognizes an allergen as foreign and attempts to attack it. For dogs, allergens may include flea bites, inhaled or skin-contacted substances (atopy), and foods.

Signs of an allergy include scratching, chewing at the fur, red skin, bumps or thickened skin, hair loss, and head shaking. Dogs are not likely to sneeze or get a runny nose from an allergy, the way we do.

Your vet will test for an allergy by taking your dog's history and doing a physical exam. He may also make a skin scraping, or order skin cytology or a complete blood count and chemistry panel. Allergy blood tests and intradermal allergy testing are also options, as are diet trials in case a food allergy is suspected. Allergies cannot be cured, only treated and managed. (If your dog is allergic to fleas, strict control is the only answer. Even one bite can set off a reaction!)

Contact Allergy

In this kind of allergy, the dog reacts to an irritant that actually touches the skin. It is not as common as AD. However, a Danish study showed that 50 percent of contact allergy- affected dogs were German Shepherd Dogs in a general population comprised of only 16 percent German Shepherd Dogs. There appears to be no age or sex predisposition.

Flea Allergy

This is one of the most common canine allergies. Some dogs start itching madly after one flea bite. The obvious way to handle it is to make sure your dog doesn't get fleas.

Food Allergies

Food allergies account for about 10 percent of all of the allergies seen in dogs and are the third most common cause of allergies after flea bite allergies and atopy (inhalant allergy). German Shepherd Dogs in particular have been reported as having a higher degree of food hypersensitivity than other dogs. Food allergies can appear as early as five months and as late as 12 years of age, though most cases occur between 2 and 6 years. Many animals with food allergies also have concurrent inhalant or contact allergies.

Dogs are most likely to be allergic to the following foods, in this order: beef, dairy products, chicken, wheat, chicken eggs, corn, and soy. These, of course, are the most common ingredients in dog foods. As lamb becomes more popular in the diet, expect to see lamb allergies show up, too. It appears that the main factor as to whether a particular food is likely to cause an allergic reaction is the structure and size of the glycoprotein in the food.

Heartworm is especially present in areas with warmer climates.

For dogs allergic to a food substance, dietary management is important. Supplementing the diet with a fatty acid also seems to help.

Hot Spots

Common in German Shepherd Dogs, these scary-looking skin sores are usually caused by irritation, allergies, or dirt in the skin. The dog will scratch himself and make the condition worse by infecting the sores. If hot spots appear, wash them thoroughly with shampoo, rinse, and dry them. You may want to use a drying powder you can obtain from your vet.

Pyoderma

Pyoderma is a staph infection of the skin, and it is the most common skin problem affecting dogs. It causes small pustules or lesions that can develop into scabs and crusts. Pyoderma usually

Theoretically, almost anything can cause an allergy, and individual dogs have shown allergic reactions to drugs, bacteria, mites, intestinal worms, ticks, fibers, floor polish, and detergents.

(but not always) produces itching and is often a symptom of a deeper problem, such as an allergy. To treat pyoderma itself, a course of oral antibiotics and frequent antibacterial shampoos over a period of three weeks are usually prescribed by a veterinarian.

Cancer

Cancer is defined as the condition of abnormal and malignant cell division and maturation. Cancer kills over half of senior dogs, but certain canine cancers develop earlier in life. Some are even hereditary.

According to the Veterinary Cancer Society, here are common signs of cancer in small animals (and notice how similar these signs are to cancer in human beings):

- Abnormal swellings that persist or continue to grow
- Bleeding or discharge from any bodily opening
- Difficulty breathing, urinating, or defecating
- Difficulty eating or swallowing
- Loss of appetite
- Offensive odor from the mouth
- Persistent lameness or stiffness
- Reluctance to exercise or loss of stamina
- Sores that don't heal
- Weight loss

While cancer can affect all mammals, one kind, hemangiosarcoma (a malignant tumor in the blood vessels of the muscles, spleen, liver, or other organs), affects German Shepherd Dogs more than any other breed. No one knows why, but it is suspected that both genetic and environmental factors play a role. The average age at which a German Shepherd Dog is affected is nine years.

GSDs also have a higher incidence of 21 other types of tumors or cancers than many other breeds. The treatment and prognosis of cancer depends on the kind and location of cancer, how soon it is discovered, and what treatments you are considering. Surgery, radiation, chemotherapy, and even gene therapy are all options, depending on the circumstances. For more information, talk to your veterinary oncologist.

Cardiovascular Disease

Like people, German Shepherd Dogs are prone to several heart conditions, including aortic stenosis, mitral dysplasia, pericardial

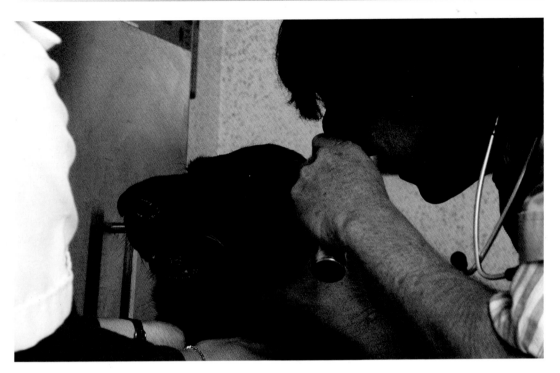

effusion, persistent left cranial vena cava, persistent right aortic arch, tricuspid dysplasia, and ventricular ectopy. You have probably never heard of most of them, and the truth is that your dog probably won't come down with any of them. Aortic stenosis is one of the most common of them, with German Shepherd Dogs at a comparatively high risk (2.6 percent) of developing the disease.

Your vet will test your GSD for allergies by taking his history and performing a complete physical exam.

Aortic Stenosis

Aortic stenosis is an inherited condition in which there is a narrowing of the heart's aortic valve or a partial obstruction of the blood flow as it leaves the left ventricle of the heart through the aorta (the main blood vessel that carries blood to the rest of the body). This is the most common heart defect in large dogs. Because of the obstruction, the heart has to work harder to pump out enough blood volume. Mild forms of the disease are not detectable and don't cause any problems for the dog. In fact, the dog will have a normal life expectancy. (However, the defect may still be passed on to offspring.)

With moderate or severe stenosis, your GSD will need to rest more, and your vet may prescribe beta blockers. Currently, this is the only viable medical treatment.

Dental Disease

Dental disease often starts with plaque, a sticky but invisible substance full of bacteria that coats the teeth, even below the gumline. Long-standing plaque develops into tartar, that hard yellow substance starting at the base of the tooth. As the bacteria population grows, the gum begins to pull away from the tooth, and a "periodontal pocket" is formed. Periodontal disease is a dangerous, unsightly, and bad-smelling infection. More dangerous bacteria fill this pocket and begin to destroy the periodontal ligament and perhaps even the jawbone. Soon the tooth can abscess or fall out.

It's a sad fact that about three quarters of all dogs aged four years and older have some form of periodontal disease. Even dogs whose conscientious owners brush their teeth regularly are at some risk. Most veterinarians recommend that dogs have their teeth professionally cleaned once a year. This cleaning procedure is done under a light general anesthesia, which is quite safe.

Halitosis (Bad Breath)

Halitosis goes by a number of fancy names, including "foetor ex ore" and "fetor oris." None of the fancy names make the dogs' breath smell any better, however. In most cases, a bad smell indicates periodontal disease resulting from the bacteria associated with plaque and calculus. Bacteria are attracted to the film that forms from saliva coating the teeth. Unless you brush your dog's teeth daily, the bacteria and plaque will mineralize, forming calculus. The rough surface of the tooth will attract even more bacteria that work their way into the gums and form pockets that accumulate decaying food particles. As the calculus ages and gingivitis and bone loss follow, bacteria change from a gram-positive aerobic type to a gram-negative anaerobic kind. It all smells bad. In most cases, the cure for bad breath is a thorough professional teeth cleaning, which will also take care of or at least halt the progression of some of the underlying problems.

In a few cases, bad breath signals dermatological, respiratory, or gastrointestinal disease.

Ear Infections

Because of their erect ears, German Shepherds are less apt to suffer from ear infections than floppy-eared breeds. However, it can happen. In fact, ear infections are one of the most common of all infections. Dogs who swim are also prone to ear infections.

The cause of ear infections is usually bacteria or yeast (*Malassezia pachydermatis*). Other causes of ear disease can include:

- Allergies
- Ear mites (*Otodectes cynotis*)
- Bacteria (many types) and yeast
- Foreign bodies, such as plant awns
- Trauma
- Hormonal problems, such as hypothyroidism
- Excess moisture in the ear
- Malformation of the ear canal
- Hereditary or immune conditions
- Tumors (squamous cell or melanoma, as well as other types)

The first signs of an ear infection may be an unpleasant odor, redness, swelling, or discharge. Other signs of ear disease include scratching, shaking, or rubbing of the ears or head, pain around the ears, and behavioral changes.

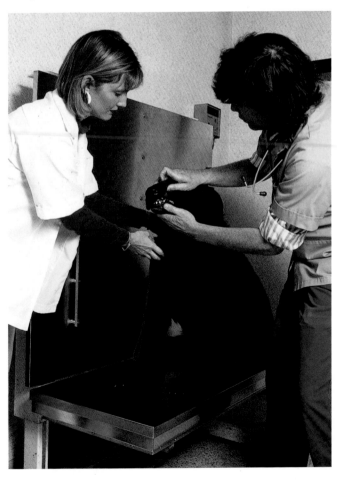

Many veterinarians recommend that dogs have their teeth professionally cleaned once a year.

Contact your vet at the first sign of an ear infection, as cases caught early are the easiest to clear up. Your vet will use an otoscope to examine the ear and if necessary will flush the ear out, probably under anesthesia. If your vet cannot find a cause, consider contacting a veterinary allergist.

Surgical treatment for ear disease is sometimes necessary when other attempts to control infection fail. One procedure facilitates treatment of the ears by allowing direct access to the horizontal canal or improving drainage. A more radical procedure, total ear canal ablation, involves actual surgical removal of the entire ear canal. If the dog has a tumor or congenital malformation of the ear canal, surgery is often the first choice. An antibiotic or antifungal medication may be used for less serious problems.

Endocrine System Disorders

Addison's Disease (Hypoadrenocorticism or Adrenocortical Insufficiency)

One of the most important diseases of the endocrine system is Addison's disease (hypoadrenocorticism), which affects the adrenal glands, found right next to the kidneys. The center (cortex) of the gland produces a group of special hormones called corticosteroids, which include mineralocorticoids such as aldosterone. These handy hormones help mammals adapt to stress. In fact, one subcategory of them, the glucocorticoids (like cortisol), are responsible for producing that all-important flight-or-flight response. Other kinds of hormones produced by the adrenal glands help balance electrolytes (sodium, potassium, and chloride) in the system. As a result, when something goes awry with the adrenal glands, your pet is in big trouble!

If you suspect your GSD is suffering from an ear infection, take him to the veterinarian immediately, as cases caught early are the easiest to clear up.

The typical Addison's patient is a female aged four to five years, although any dog of any age may be affected. Signs may include lethargy, lack of appetite, vomiting, or diarrhea, but they are vague, intermittent, and various. This is one reason that Addison's is called "the great imitator." Your vet needs to perform a special test called the ACTH stimulation test to be sure.

If left unnoticed or untreated, your dog will experience an "Addisonian crisis" in which his blood sugar will drop dangerously low and the imbalance of electrolytes will disrupt the heart rhythm. Untreated dogs usually die. Fortunately, the disease can be managed with medications. Treatment includes replacing the missing mineralocorticoid hormones. Your vet will be able to prescribe the right medication for your particular dog, but in any case, he must remain on it for life. Common medications for Addison's include low-dose prednisone (to replace the cortisone). The aldosterone can be replaced by a daily oral medication or a monthly injectable. The injectable medication is less expensive than the oral treatment, but neither is cheap. Addison's dogs need careful monitoring, and if they receive it, they can live a full and fairly normal life.

Look for the Seal

The Seal of Acceptance from the Veterinary Oral Health Council appears on products that meet defined standards for plaque and tartar control in dogs and cats.

Cushing's Disease (Hyperadrenocorticism)

This disease is caused by the production of too much adrenal hormone, specifically corticosteroids. In some cases, the precipitating cause is a tumor either in the adrenal gland itself or more commonly in the pituitary gland, which stimulates the adrenal gland to produce hormones. GSDs are more prone to this condition than some other breeds.

Signs of Cushing's disease include excessive thirst, increased urination, panting, symmetrical hair loss, skin infections, and high blood pressure. Several blood tests are used to diagnose the disease, notably the low-dose dexamethasone test. Once the disease is diagnosed, the high-dose dexamethasone suppression test is performed to distinguish the kind of tumor involved. An adrenal gland tumor can sometimes be removed, but pituitary tumors are generally left in place. The disease is then treated (but not cured) with mitotane, the dosage of which must be carefully regulated.

Diabetes Mellitus

Diabetes mellitus is a chronic condition in which the body doesn't produce enough insulin (referred to as "congenital" or "Type 1"), or something interferes with the insulin's ability to be utilized by the body (referred to as "acquired" or "Type 2"). Insulin is a hormone that helps the body to metabolize sugar. Diabetes in dogs is most commonly the acquired form and usually affects middle-aged animals of either sex. The cause is unknown, but obese dogs and females are at greater risk.

A diabetic dog has too much glucose in the bloodstream (where most of it cannot be used) and not enough glucose within the cells themselves, where it is most needed for energy. To compensate, the

If your Shepherd has been diagnosed with diabetes, he can still live a full life under your diligent care.

cells attempt to get energy in other ways, such as from fat breakdown. This in turn leads to the production of harmful by-products called ketones. The accumulation of ketones makes the blood more acidic (ketoacidosis), a condition in which normal metabolic functions begin to fail. Diabetes can be life-threatening and requires aggressive medical therapy. Signs of diabetes include increased thirst and urination and weight loss despite a good appetite.

Your vet can diagnose the disease by doing a medical history, physical examination, and urinalysis to check for glucose. An analysis of the blood to determine the glucose concentration, and a serum biochemical profile may also be performed. Diabetes cannot be cured, but it can be treated with daily insulin. Oral insulin can sometimes be given at first, but eventually your dog will probably require injections that you can give at home. Regular administration of insulin and establishing regular feeding times are very important.

At first, it may be difficult to find the proper amount of insulin to give your dog, and in the beginning you may need to make frequent trips to the vet. You might even have to have your dog stay at the hospital so that the vet can map out a glucose curve, a chart that shows the rising and falling levels of glucose in the blood. Weight control, fiber in the diet, and regular exercise are also important in controlling diabetes.

Of course, it's much better to keep your dog thin, thus helping to prevent diabetes from occurring in the first place. Feeding your dog an appropriate amount for his life stage and activity level and providing adequate exercise can keep him at an ideal weight.

Hypothyroidism

Hypothyroidism is the most common hormonal disorder in dogs who are between four and ten years of age, although it often crops up during puberty. As its name indicates, hypothyroidism is a disorder of the thyroid gland, which is located in the neck. The thyroid gland produces the hormone thyroxine, which regulates the metabolic rate in many different tissues. In dogs who are suffering from hypothyroidism, not enough thyroxine is produced, which causes the metabolism in these tissues to slow down. Most cases result from an immune-mediated process that develops in genetically susceptible dogs.

Signs of hypothyroidism include lethargy, depression, exercise intolerance, obesity, digestive disorders, cold intolerance, and skin disorders, especially a thin, harsh coat with symmetrical hair loss.

Clear, shiny eyes are indicative of good health; anything unusual should be reported to your veterinarian.

Diagnosis can be complicated, involving a complete blood count, chemistry panel, urinalysis, thyroxine level test, or a thyroid stimulating hormone (TSH) test. Treatment is usually just a daily oral dose of synthetic thyroxine, which must be continued for the rest of the dog's life.

Eye Diseases

German Shepherd dogs have been reported as having a higher-than-usual incidence of a variety of eye defects, in addition to other diseases that are common in all breeds.

Cataracts

Cataracts are unfortunately rather common in German Shepherd Dogs. While dogs can develop cataracts, just as humans can, there is new hope for their treatment, thanks to computer-aided technology that allows veterinarians to make a tiny incision in the dog's cornea. A small probe emits ultrasonic waves that break up the diseased lens,

and a foldable synthetic replacement is then inserted. Old-fashioned cataract surgery required two incisions: one to remove the lens and another to insert the replacement. The new procedure decreases inflammation, pain, and complications and has a success rate of over 90 percent.

Dry Eye (keratoconjunctivitis sicca)

Dry eye is a deficiency of tears that results in the drying and inflammation of the cornea and conjunctiva. It is very common in dogs and is probably an inherited disease. It may also be related to allergies but can result from other factors, such as immune-mediated adenitis, trauma, or a systemic disease like distemper.

The most common medication and treatment of choice for dry eye is cyclosporine (0.2 percent), a drug that uses immunosuppression as its primary mode of action.

Signs of hypothyroidism include lethargy and depression, as well as exercise intolerance and various digestive disorders.

Pannus (Uberreiter's disease)

Pannus is a chronic inflammation of the corneal surface and conjunctiva of the eye. It first appears in the outer areas of the cornea and almost always affects both eyes simultaneously. It

generally shows up in dogs between three and five years of age and is a common ailment of the German Shepherd Dog.

Pannus is treated with antibiotics and antiviral and antimycotic agents as appropriate. As pannus is an immune-mediated disease, it is even more commonly treated with cyclosporine and steroids. In some cases, treatment must be continued throughout the life of the dog.

Gastrointestinal Disorders

German Shepherd Dogs have a higher-than-normal incidence of many gastrointestinal conditions, not counting the ones that all dogs are prone to.

Diarrhea

Diarrhea is really a sign of a disease rather than a disease itself. The precipitating cause may be as benign as a change in diet or something more serious, like an illness. In general, most dogs with diarrhea do best if they are not given any food for 24 hours after the episode to give their digestive tract a rest. Fluids containing an electrolyte solution can be given.

When you begin to feed your dog again, select a light, nutritious, highly digestible diet like chicken and rice in small, frequent meals. It's best to give a diet with a single-source meat protein and a single-source carbohydrate supplemented with correctly balanced vitamins and minerals. For simple diarrhea, Kaopectate (about 2cc/kg every 4-6 hours) or Pepto-Bismol (2cc/kg every 4-6 hours) administered orally may also be helpful. Herbalists often use slippery elm with good effect. Once your dog has recovered, you can gradually go back to his normal diet over a period of three to four days. If the diarrhea continues for a day or two after a 24-hour fast, a trip to the vet is in order.

Bloody diarrhea may be relatively minor or very serious. Top suspects include parasite infection, a large or sharp object lodged in the intestine, or even a change in diet! In any case, your vet will need to examine your dog, so be sure to bring a stool sample.

Gastroenteritis

Gastritis is an inflammation of the stomach, and enteritis is an inflammation of the bowels. Thus, gastroenteritis (you got it!) is an

Appetite Loss

Loss of appetite is frequently a sign of some other problem. While healthy dogs can miss a couple of meals without suffering, a longer fasting period indicates something could be seriously wrong. The culprit could be periodontal disease or even a broken tooth. It could also be a viral disease, a hormonal disorder, cancer, or heart disease. It could even be depression or anxiety. If your dog loses his appetite, please take him to the vet for a thorough evaluation.

inflammation of a major portion of the intestinal tract.

This condition can be caused by numerous factors, including infection, liver disease, eating bad food, medications, or even allergies. When the gastrointestinal tract becomes inflamed, the normal process of digestion is disturbed, resulting in vomiting, diarrhea, and consequent dehydration.

To treat gastroenteritis, your vet may prescribe oral or intravenous fluid therapy, as well as antibiotics or drugs to control vomiting.

Vomiting

Vomiting is a sign of many different conditions and diseases—anything from dietary indiscretion or spoiled food to ingested objects, worms, ulcers, and a host of serious diseases. If your dog begins to vomit, withhold food and limit his water intake for 24 hours. If he continues to vomit after this point, call your vet immediately.

Drinking from unfamiliar and potentially unsafe sources can lead to stomach upset or worse.

Kidney (Renal) Disease

Healthy kidneys keep in balance the body's chemical reactions, blood pressure, acid-base balance, mineral levels, and elimination of waste products. They can be damaged by bacterial infections (such as leptospirosis and Lyme disease, or common bacteria, like proteus and staph). Kidney disease can also be inherited. A kidney can develop tumors, become injured by toxins like antifreeze, and so on. You probably won't know your dog has kidney disease until it is well advanced, because symptoms don't appear until about 80 percent of kidney function has been lost. Signs include excessive thirst, frequent urination, and very dilute urine. Weight loss, vomiting, and depression may follow.

Kidney disease has many causes, but in most cases the treatment is the same—more fluids and less protein, phosphorus, and salt. Sometimes B vitamins, iron, or calcitriol is supplemented. Holistic practitioners often suggest the addition of fish oil (a source of omega-3 fatty acids) to the diet. Herbalists may treat kidney disease with a preparation of rhubarb (Rheum officinale), and homeopaths may use a preparation of Kali chloricum.

Nervous System Disorders

The nervous system is the headquarters of your dog's behavior and movement, so it is crucial that everything functions properly in this area!

Canine Cognitive Dysfunction (CCD)

According to Pfizer Pharmaceutical, 62 percent of dogs aged ten years and older may develop signs of canine cognitive dysfunction (CCD). These include:

- Confusion or disorientation. (The dog may get lost in his own back yard or become trapped in corners or behind furniture.)
- Forgetting housetraining abilities.
- Maintaining lower levels of activity.
- Not recognizing people or other pets.
- Pacing, lying awake all night, or changes in sleeping patterns.
- Staring vaguely into space.

Luckily, there is medication available that can successfully manage this condition. Talk to your vet to discover your options.

Your Senior GSD

Dogs aged 10 or older are considered senior citizens and need extra care and attention. Just like us, their bodies and minds change. Be attentive to their needs.

Epilepsy

In dogs who suffer from epilepsy, there is abnormal electrical activity in the brain that interferes with nerve transmission. The dog cannot use his muscles properly during the seizure, resulting in involuntary contractions of the muscles that compose a seizure. The first seizure usually occurs between one and seven years of age.

Primary epilepsy is a condition characterized by seizures of unknown (idiopathic) origin. When it is known what is causing the seizures, the disease is referred to as secondary epilepsy, which can be caused by such things as hypoglycemia (low blood sugar), liver problems, poisoning, heart problems, infection, and cancer. Blood tests, x-rays, electrocardiograms, ultrasounds, MRIs, and other tests may rule out these other conditions.

A classic epileptic event has several stages. The first stage, or aura, precedes the event itself. During this stage, the dog may try to hide from or stay very close to the owner; he may even become aggressive.

The seizure itself is called the ictus or crisis stage. A seizure is a scary event to observe, one that is even more distressing to the owner than to the dog. In a generalized seizure (tonic-clonic), all of the skeletal muscles contract, and the dog loses consciousness. He will fall to his side with his head thrown back and legs stretched out. He may vocalize, twitch, urinate, defecate, or drool. This part of the seizure is called the tonic phase. In the clonic phase, which usually occurs right after the tonic phase, the dog will jerk rhythmically (perhaps look like he's running) and clench his jaws. During the crisis, or ictus, take care to prevent the dog from hurting himself. Remove furniture in close proximity to your pet, and prevent the animal from falling downstairs. Do not try to put your hands in his mouth, as you can be bitten very badly. The best thing you can do for your dog at this time is to be quiet, dim the room if you can, and keep other pets away. Time the seizure and keep records. Call your vet after it is over to ask for an appointment and consultation.

Owners of epileptic dogs need to monitor them and recognize warning signs of seizures.

During the post-ictal period, the dog will lie quite still and then get up, usually showing some aftereffects of the seizure, such as disorientation or passing out. Unfortunately, this phase can last for hours or even longer. In between episodes, the pet will appear normal, both physically and mentally. Not all seizures are so dramatic, though. In a partial seizure, only a part of the body, such as the head, may be affected. A partial seizure probably has a specific cause, unlike many cases of generalized epilepsy.

Many drugs are available to control epilepsy, although the disease has no cure and treatment is for life. The goal of drug therapy is to reduce the intensity, frequency, and duration of the seizures. By giving the appropriate medication at the right dosage, the condition will be well controlled in most pets.

Skeletal Diseases

Without a skeleton that functions properly, your dog isn't going anywhere. As a result, diseases of this vital system are a cause for concern.

Arthritis

If your dog has arthritis, he is not alone; in fact, he has 10 million fellow sufferers. Arthritis, formally known as osteoarthritis, is simply the inflammation of a joint, typically the synovial joints, which consist of two bones and a fibrous capsule (a sort of hinge) filled with synovial fluid that holds them together. The surfaces of the bones are covered with slippery cartilage that helps the bones glide over each other during normal movement. Because arthritis can be caused by an injury, normal wear and tear, bad conformation, joint abnormalities, and even tick-borne diseases, many dogs are potential victims.

A regimen of nutritional support and pain relief medication can go a long way to help an arthritic dog.

In dogs who are afflicted with arthritis, the cartilage becomes rough and worn. The joint capsule becomes inflamed, and the lubricating fluid it produces stops working well. The key signs are stiffness and a limited range of motion. However, never simply assume that a stiff dog has arthritis. A number of other, more serious conditions, such as bone infections, tumors, fractures, and dysplasia, can mimic its signs. Get an accurate diagnosis from your veterinarian first before proceeding with the appropriate treatment.

Care of an arthritic dog involves the regular use of pain relievers, such as oral nonsteroidal anti-inflammatory drugs (NSAIDs) like carpofen; polysulfated glycosaminoglycan given by injection twice a week to help with pain, reduce inflammation, and rebuild damaged cartilage; a buffered aspirin formulated specifically for dogs; and newer generations of medications. Some of these drugs may cause intestinal bleeding, and a few dogs develop liver or kidney problems from their

Older dogs—especially those who are still active—can benefit from supplements and medication to relieve joint pain.

use. As a result, dogs on NSAIDs should be carefully monitored.

Glucosamine/chondroitin supplements with manganese are very effective as well. Studies show they are as effective as NSAIDs for arthritis, with very few of the side effects. (There is a concern, however, that glucosamine may reduce the blood's ability to clot, which would be dangerous for a dog with von Willebrand's disease.) They do take four to eight weeks to become effective. Glucosamine, a building block for cartilage, is produced naturally in the body. Commercial glucosamine, derived from the shells of shrimp, comes in several forms, but the most effective for treating arthritis are glucosamine hydrochloride and glucosamine sulfate. Glucosamine is rapidly taken up by cartilage cells and helps in the synthesis of synovial fluid. Chondroitin is also a naturally produced substance; it works to stymie enzymes that cause joint pain. This substance works especially well for older dogs, whose natural production of chondroitin has declined with age. Glucosamine and chondroitin together help reduce swelling and improve circulation, in addition to their other benefits. Be sure to get a product that includes manganese; it is a necessary cofactor for the biosynthesis of glycosaminoglycans. As a bonus, look for a product with ascorbate, a necessary cofactor for collagen biosynthesis. However, many of the brands sold over the counter do not contain the amount of the supplement that they claim. To be certain, talk to your veterinarian about obtaining a prescription for a veterinary-quality supplement.

Research indicates that green-lipped mussel contains a supplement that may help both osteoarthritis and rheumatoid arthritis. It contains natural anti-inflammatory agents and building blocks to rebuild certain joint components.

Degenerative Myelopathy

This progressive rear limb weakness or paralysis is of great concern to German Shepherd Dog owners, as it is very common in this breed while comparatively rare in others. The age of onset is usually between 5 and 14 years.

Over time, the patient will become progressively weaker, and the dog will develop a characteristic "shuffling" of the rear legs as well as a lack of coordination. Eventually, full paralysis coupled with fecal and urinary incontinence will develop.

Unfortunately, there is no medical or surgical treatment available. The only solution is to keep your dog as active and thin as possible for as long as possible.

Hip Check

German Shepherds are especially prone to hip dysplasia. Learn its signs and symptoms and work with your veterinarian to possibly prevent or at least minimize its incidence in your dog.

Hip Dysplasia

This crippling disease of growing dogs is due to an abnormal development of the hip joint—the head of the femur does not fit properly into its socket. Some cases are fairly mild, while others are excruciatingly painful. German Shepherd Dogs are genetically predisposed to this disease, but other factors, including growth rate, diet, and weight gain can also be involved. Some dogs show signs of the disease as puppies, while others don't until old age, even though the disease has been present all along.

Signs of hip dysplasia include:
- Abnormal gait (like a "bunny hop")
- Lameness
- Swaying or staggering
- Reluctance to climb stairs
- Difficulty in getting up

The disease can be confirmed with x-rays, which in young dogs may require sedation or anesthesia. There are several ways to treat hip dysplasia, such as helping your dog lose weight, ensuring he gets proper exercise (such as swimming), administering pain relievers, and surgery. The type of surgery depends on the age of the dog and other factors, such as the degree and type of dysplasia. Popular surgeries include a triple pelvic osteotomy (TPO), femoral head and neck ostectomy (FHO), and total hip replacement (THR).

Hip dysplasia can be eliminated from the canine population by only breeding dogs who have a clearance from the Orthopedic Foundation for Animals (OFA). In addition, the PennHIP program for evaluating canine hips can provide excellent, objective information about hip joints in puppies and dogs as young as four months of age.

Elbow Dysplasia

Elbow dysplasia is the forelimb counterpart to hip dysplasia, but unlike hip dysplasia, it has only been recognized as a problem in the last few decades. Elbow dysplasia can take four different forms: ununited anconeal process, osteochondrodystrophy (OCD) of the distal humeral condyle, fragmented medial coronoid process, and elbow incongruity. Any dog might have just one or all four of these forms. Dogs with elbow dysplasia are lame in one or both front legs.

Surgery can correct the problem, but the dog will require cage rest for four to six weeks afterward. That is the toughest part! Depending on the exact type of dysplasia your GSD has, other therapies and medications may be available. Consult your veterinarian for more information.

CANINE EMERGENCIES

An emergency is a situation in which you need to get your dog to the vet as quickly as possible. Of course, not every ailment needs professional treatment, and even professional treatment can sometimes be scheduled somewhat at your leisure. However, the following symptoms require immediate action:

- Bleeding from the nose or mouth
- Broken bones

Anal Sac Problems

The anal sacs are located on both sides of the anus, just under the skin. They produce a dark, smelly fluid (related to the chemical a skunk emits) that connects to the anus via tiny ducts. In a normal civilized life, a dog has scant reason to empty the sacs, and so they can become impacted, infected, or abscessed. If your dog is having anal sac trouble, you may see him "scoot" along the ground and incorrectly surmise he has worms. He may also lick under his tail. The area itself may be swollen, painful, or have a bloody or purulent discharge.

Simple impaction, in which there is no redness or swelling, can be relieved by emptying the sacs and cleaning out the solidified material. Infections require antibiotics, and abscesses need surgery. Your veterinarian is the best person to advise you of the proper course of treatment for your dog. If the sacs continue to cause trouble, your vet can perform surgery to remove them.

- Bloated abdomen
- Pale gums
- Diarrhea lasting more than 18 hours
- Muscle tremors
- Problems with breathing or swallowing
- Refusal to eat for 48 hours
- Repeated vomiting
- Seizures or disorientation
- Spurting blood (arterial bleeding)
- Unusual swellings, especially sudden, hard, or fast-growing ones

Bites and Stings

Creepy crawlies are everywhere, and your curious German Shepherd is more than likely to have a run-in with a bee, hornet, wasp, centipede or spider sooner or later.

Most insect stings leave a painful swelling around the site. If the stinger is still in place, scrape it away with a credit card, or gently remove it with tweezers. To relieve pain and itching, make a paste of baking soda and water to apply to the area, or use a commercial product. A cold compress may also help. (You can even use a bag of frozen peas!) Bee stings in the mouth can be treated by giving your dog ice chips to chew to cool the area. You can also try to flush the area with a mixture of 1 teaspoon of baking soda and enough water to make a thin paste (using a turkey baster), but don't let him inhale the stuff.

Beware the critters who may bite and sting your friend while outside.

If a poisonous spider has bitten your dog, he'll need veterinary care. Apply an ice pack or cold compress to the area to slow the spread of venom, and get him to the vet right away. Untreated dogs can go into shock and die. You should also immediately transport your dog to the vet if he shows signs of an allergic reaction, such as hives or difficulty breathing.

Bleeding

If your German Shepherd Dog is bleeding, your job is to apply pressure to staunch it. Use towels or clean rags, and keep pressing until the bleeding stops. Resist the urge to pull off the cloth—you'll just remove the scab that is forming.

Much more serious than regular cuts, of course, are cuts that

slice across arteries. Arterial blood is usually bright red and comes in spurts, rather than the steady flow of darker blood characteristic of surface or venous cuts. In cases of arterial bleeding, you must stop the blood flow at once. Apply strong pressure to the blood flow. If the bleeding continues, apply pressure to the pressure point closest to the wound, between the wound and the heart. Pressure points are located in the "armpits," the groin, and just below the base on the underside of the tail. Press firmly until the bleeding slows. You will have to relax the pressure for a few seconds every few minutes so that you don't cause tissue and nerve death. If there is a lot of blood, take your dog to the vet immediately.

A careful going-over of your dog with your fingers can reveal the source of an injury.

Bloat (Gastric Torsion and Stomach Distension)

Bloat is a serious, life-threatening emergency. It must be treated by a veterinarian *immediately* to save the life of your dog. German Shepherd Dogs are at high risk of bloat, as are many other large, deep-chested breeds.

The technical name for this terrible condition is gastric dilatation volvulus (GDV). When a dog is afflicted with bloat, gases or air build up in the stomach, typically after a large meal. The technical name for this expansion is dilatation, but "bloat" says it all. After a certain point, the stomach twists more than 180 degrees on its long axis (this is called torsion), cutting off contact with the esophagus and trapping the gas so the dog can't belch or pass gas. This puts pressure on the large blood vessels of the abdomen, leading ultimately to organ failure. The stomach may even rupture. In addition, digestion ceases at this point, causing fermenting food and bacteria to accumulate in the stomach, bringing about tissue death. The food and bacteria can even get into the bloodstream, forming clots and perhaps pushing the dog into shock.

This disease attacks suddenly and often at night. A stricken dog can die within two hours of onset, and more than one owner has come home to the tragic sight of a dog killed by bloat. It is an agonizing and painful death. Symptoms of bloat include:

- Unsuccessful attempts to vomit
- Extended abdomen in most cases as the condition progresses
- Pacing and discomfort
- Pale mucous membranes
- Panting
- Repeatedly lying down and getting back up
- Salivation

These signs indicate an emergency. Get your German Shepherd to the emergency vet clinic immediately, even if it's 3:00 a.m. Do not wait. If left untreated even for a few hours, your dog will probably die. The first 20 to 30 minutes are most critical. If you arrive at the animal hospital in time, the vet may be able to insert a tube down the dog's stomach to release the gases if torsion has not occurred. (This can be confirmed by an x-ray.) The dog will be treated for shock and made ready for surgery. If torsion has occurred, the vet may insert a tube directly through the abdominal wall into the stomach. Once the situation is stabilized, the vet will perform surgery to reposition the stomach.

Gastropexy is the treatment of choice when a dog is subjected to one or more bouts of bloat. In this surgical procedure, the vet will stitch the stomach to the abdominal wall in an attempt to prevent it from twisting. This procedure will not stop bloat, but it will prevent the accompanying torsion. Even the best treatment does not assure success, though. Animals who have a lot of dead tissue or who have suffered cardiac complications are at increased risk of death or at least a long and difficult recovery.

No one really knows what causes bloat or how to prevent it. Many factors combine to create a risk environment for the disease. They include breed, size and shape of the dog, age, genetics, diet,

Your Canine First-Aid Kit

Although you can buy a basic commercial kit, it's cheaper and more fun to make one yourself. First, you need a box—a fishing tackle or other shoebox-sized container is perfect. It should be strong, waterproof, and unlocked. Try to get one with a handle. Label it "First Aid" with a felt-tip pen on all sides. Keep it in plain view. Under the lid, tape an index card with the name, number, and hours of your vet and poison control center. Also, write down the name, description, and weight of each of your animals. In case you are not home when disaster strikes, your pet sitter will thank you. Put an emergency blanket under the first-aid kit, and keep one in the car as well. It will help prevent shock by preserving the animal's heat.

- **Activated Charcoal:** For poisonings (1 gram per pound mixed with water).
- **Antihistamine tablets:** For insect stings and allergic reactions.
- **Betadine or Nolvasan:** Cleaning open wounds.
- **Blunt-nosed scissors:** To cut tape and clip hair. Keep these scissors with the kit, and don't take them out to use for anything else. You may not put them back, and when you need them, you'll wonder where they are.
- **Canine rectal thermometer:** For taking your dog's temperature.
- **Cortisone ointment:** Topical anti-inflammatory.
- **Cotton balls and swabs:** Various uses, such as cleaning wounds.
- **Eyedropper or dosage syringe:** To apply medication.
- **Eyewash:** To irrigate eyes.
- **First-aid cream:** To soothe and protect wounds.
- **Gloves:** Two pairs—one set of thin plastic gloves to avoid contamination, and heavy gloves if you fear being bitten.
- **Hand towel:** Cleaning up, drying hands, etc.
- **Hydrogen peroxide (3 percent):** Various uses, such as for inducing vomiting.
- **Ipecac or hydrogen peroxide:** To induce vomiting (1 teaspoon per 20 pounds).
- **Kaolin and pectin:** To help diarrhea (1 teaspoon per 10 pounds).
- **Magnifying Glass:** To locate tiny objects.
- **Muzzle:** If you don't have one, you can make one from nylons or a strip of fabric.
- **Nail Clippers:** In case of an accident to the nail bed.
- **Nonstick adhesive tape:** For taping bandages.
- **Nonstinging antiseptic spray or swabs:** For cleaning wounds.
- **Pepto-Bismol or Maalox:** Stomach coater for minor intestinal upset.
- **Petroleum jelly:** To accompany the rectal thermometer, also for constipation (1/2 teaspoon per 10 pounds).
- **Saline solution:** Various uses, such as irrigating wounds.
- **Stretch bandage:** For wounds.
- **Styptic pencil:** To stop minor bleeding.
- **Tweezers or hemostat:** To pull out splinters and other foreign objects.
- **Two rolls of 3-inch gauze bandages:** For wrapping wounds.
- **Vegetable oil:** For mild constipation (1 teaspoon per 5 pounds, mixed in with food).

and (rather surprisingly) personality. Fortunately, some basic dietary precautions can help prevent the disease:

- Divide your dog's meals into smaller meals served over the course of the day.
- Wait an hour after a meal before vigorously exercising your dog.
- Add canned food or table scraps if you serve kibble.
- Do not use a raised bowl.
- Keep your dog happy and at the proper weight.
- Consider adding a human anti-gas product containing simethicone to his meal.

Heatstroke and Heat Exhaustion

A dog's normal body temperature ranges from 100.5°F to 102.5°F. If a dog is suffering from heatstroke, his body temperature will rise to the point where he is unable to cool himself. When the body temperature rises to 103°F to 105°F degrees, the condition is called heat exhaustion. Heatstroke occurs when body temperature rises above 106°F. (This kind of body temperature elevation is different from that produced by fever or infection, but it is just as serious.)

Be careful not to overwork your dog on a hot day.

We human beings have sweat glands all over the surface of our skin, but dogs have very few sweat glands, mostly located in the footpads. They must cool themselves by panting, a process in which the moist lining of the lungs works as the evaporative surface. (Dogs do not have sweat glands in their tongues!) Dogs can also dissipate some heat by dilating blood vessels in their ears, which makes the blood flow closer to the surface of the skin. If your dog becomes overheated, his body can no longer accommodate the excessive heat, and multi-system organ dysfunction results.

Heat exhaustion or heatstroke can occur after overexertion or by leaving a dog in a parked car (even with the windows partly open). It can occur within just a few minutes. Both heatstroke and heat exhaustion can cause brain damage, heart

To prevent heatstroke, make sure your dog has access to plenty of cool water when exerting himself outdoors.

failure, or even death very quickly. Suspect heatstroke if your German Shepherd Dog pants and salivates excessively in the hot weather and has red, staring, glassy eyes or seems confused. A seriously affected dog may vomit or even have convulsions.

If you suspect your dog has heatstroke, wet him down with wet, cool (not cold) towels and fan him. Very cold water will contract the surface blood vessels and lock the heat inside. Get him to the vet as soon as possible, even if he seems better.

To prevent heatstroke, keep your dog indoors in blazing hot weather. If he is outside, you can provide a child's wading pool, which most dogs enjoy. Limit his exercise on hot days, keeping walks to early morning and after sunset. (Remember that dogs are essentially "barefoot" and can burn their paws on hot pavement.)

Hypothermia

The opposite of heatstroke is hypothermia. This occurs when the dog's temperature drops below 96°F. Any sign that your dog is cold, such as shivering, should tell you to bring him inside immediately. After you have brought him indoors, keep him quiet to prevent lethal cardiac arrhythmia, and rewarm him gradually. Serious cases require veterinary attention and "core rewarming" techniques, which may include warm water gastric and peritoneal lavage. In milder cases, thermal insulation with blankets may help. Do not attempt to warm the limbs, because the blood will rush to the limbs, leaving the core of the body in the process and shutting down essential functions. Get your dog to the vet as soon as possible.

Inability to Breathe

Dogs who have stopped breathing may respond to cardiopulmonary resuscitation (CPR), and to be effective, it must be administered quickly. When performing CPR, you are giving your dog artificial respiration and chest compressions to get his heart going at the same time. If possible, it's best to have two people working: one for the breathing and one for the heart. Of course, that's not always possible. The chances of its success aren't great, but it is better than nothing. Also, no national standards for canine CPR exist, so guidelines vary.

A dog who needs CPR will be unconscious. You cannot perform CPR on a conscious dog. For one thing, it's ineffective and dangerous for the dog. For another, you'll be bitten. CPR works using the ABC method: airway, breathing, and circulation.

Canine CPR

Hopefully you will never need to use the lifesaving method of cardiopulmonary resuscitation on your—or any—dog. But just in case, learn the steps, and be prepared.

"A" Is for Airway

If your dog is not breathing, the first thing you need to do is to establish a clear airway. Carefully pull the tongue out of the animal's mouth. Use gloves—a dog who is almost unconscious may bite instinctively. Bring the head in line with the neck, but don't pull if there is trauma to the neck area. Visually inspect to see if the airway is open. If you see a foreign body, put your finger in the back of the mouth above the tongue and sweep the object upward. If the object remains stuck, lift the dog upside down with his back to your chest, and give several sharp thrusts just below the dog's rib cage to expel it.

Close the mouth and do two rescue breaths (your mouth to his nose). If you are able to breathe into the nose with no obstructions, go to B. If you encounter problems, reposition the neck and look down the throat for foreign bodies. If you see any, reach in and attempt to extract them. If that doesn't work, try the Heimlich maneuver: pick up the hind legs, holding your dog upside down, with his back against your chest. With your arms, give the dog five sharp thrusts to the abdomen to expel the object.

If you think your pet has been poisoned, call your vet or the ASPCA National Animal Poison Control Center at (900) 443-0000 immediately. The charge is billed directly to the caller's phone. You can also call (888) 4ANI-HELP ((888) 426-4435), billed to the caller's credit card only. Follow-up calls can be made for no additional charge by dialing (888) 299-2973.

"B" Is for Breathing

Look and listen for signs of breathing. If there are none, place your hands around the dog's muzzle to prevent air from escaping through the side of the mouth, and breathe forcefully into the nostrils. The chest should expand and fall if you are getting air into the lungs. Rescue breathing should be given at a rate of eight to ten breaths per minute (or one breath every six seconds). Get your dog to the vet as soon as possible after he is breathing on his own.

"C" Is for Circulation

If there is no pulse, place the dog on a hard surface with his right side down. Use the heel of your hand to compress the chest on the lower side right behind the elbow. The compression should be firm and not a sudden blow. It helps to have two people: the first gives the cardiac massage, while the second does the breathing. CPR should be given at a rate of 80 to 120 compressions per minute, with 2 ventilations being given every 15 compressions of the chest.

Poisoning

If you suspect your German Shepherd Dog has been poisoned, check the label on the product if possible, and read what it has to say about toxicity. The treatment will vary depending on the poison and whether it has been ingested, inhaled, or absorbed through the skin. If there's a number on the package, call to get more details. Then, call your vet or poison control center right away. Be able to provide the name of the poison; how much was absorbed, ingested, or inhaled; how long has passed since the event; how much your GSD weighs; and the signs of poisoning your pet is displaying. If your German Shepherd Dog is vomiting or has diarrhea, take samples to the vet to help with a diagnosis. Take the container that may have held the poisonous substance as well.

All poisonings should be treated as emergencies. If the exposure is to a topical poison, bathe the affected area in lukewarm running water with mild soap. If the poison is ingested, call your vet; you may be able to induce vomiting if the incident occurred less than two hours previously. (Don't induce vomiting if the dog has eaten a corrosive substance). You may also be able to give the dog some activated charcoal to delay absorption and bind the toxin.

The Healthy German Shepherd Dog

As a responsible dog owner, your job is to know the signs of sickness and health in your pet. If your German Shepherd doesn't appear normal based on the following indicators, give your vet a call, describe the signs, and follow her advice.

Temperature: 100.5°F to 102.5°F (38.1°C to 39.2°C)

Respiratory Rate: 15 to 20 breaths a minutes. *Danger signs:* Irregular breathing, shortness of breath, prolonged or heavy panting.

Heart Rate: 80 to 120 beats per minute.

Gums and Mucous Membranes: Pink. *Danger signs:* Pale, yellow, dark red, or purplish gums.

Ears: Clean and clean smelling. *Danger signs:* Discharge, debris, odor, redness, swelling, twitching, scratching, or shaking.

Nose: Clean. *Danger Signs:* Running, crusting, or discharge.

Hair Coat: Full. *Danger signs:* Wounds, lumps, hair loss, dander.

Eyes: Clear and bright. *Danger signs:* Swelling, redness, or discharge.

Capillary Refill Time: Press on your dog's gum. The spot should fill back in within a couple of seconds.

Hydration: To check if your dog is adequately hydrated, grasp the skin on his neck between your fingers, pull up, and hold it for five seconds. Then release. If it takes more than five seconds for it to return to its original position, he is probably dehydrated.

Seizures

A seizure occurs when the neurons in the brain fire uncontrollably. A seizure usually lasts between 30 seconds and several minutes, with longer seizures being very dangerous. (Also refer to the section on Epilepsy earlier in this chapter.)

Causes of seizures can include tumors, cardiovascular disease, trauma, liver or kidney disease, infections, neurological malfunction, or toxins. When no cause for the seizure can be determined, it is called idiopathic epilepsy.

Dogs usually seem to be aware of an approaching seizure, and exhibit typical signs such as restlessness or confusion, licking of the lips (often a sign of anxiety in dogs), and twitching. During the seizure itself, dogs may display partial or total loss of consciousness, involuntary "paddling" or running leg movements, twitching or shaking, excessive salivation, and involuntary voiding of feces or urine.

There is nothing you can do in the way of first aid to shorten a seizure or lessen its severity, except to keep the area quiet and dim. Prevent the dog from injuring himself by moving any furniture or other heavy objects out of his reach. Afterward, the dog may seem

Help stabilize a dog who may be unsteady.

confused or disoriented. He may seem especially in need of attention, too. This behavior may go on for a day or so after the seizure.

It is important that you seek veterinary aid after the seizure has passed, especially if it goes on for more than five minutes. Your vet will perform a physical exam to try to determine possible underlying diseases. If the first tests don't reveal an obvious cause, the next series of tests may include a complete neurological examination of brain stem function, an electroencephalogram (EEG), which records activity in the brain, and a complete blood count. A diagnosis of epilepsy usually means that no specific cause for the seizures has been found.

The anticonvulsant prescribed most often for seizures is phenobarbital. It is highly effective, affordable, and easily administered by pill, liquid, or injection. Other drugs, such as potassium bromide, may also be used. Your dog will be monitored to record the number and strength of any subsequent seizures, and his medication will be adjusted accordingly. If your dog has been diagnosed with epilepsy, don't change his medication without consulting your vet, and be sure to take your dog regularly for follow-up visits (at least once a year).

Stroke

Once it was believed that dogs didn't have strokes. Today, we know better, and even a mild stroke is considered an emergency. As with humans, strokes in dogs occur when there is a hemorrhage or blood clot in a vessel in the brain. The part of the brain supplied by the blood vessel begins to die.

Signs of stroke include leg weakness and facial paralysis on one side of the body. The dog may also lose bladder control or even consciousness. Sometimes a dog may become suddenly blind. In most cases, however, the dog will begin to recover within a short period, and a few months later he will be as good as new.

If your vet suspects a stroke, he will put your dog in an "oxygen tent" (which for dogs is really more like a cage) and use drugs to dissolve the clots in the brain. Physical therapy may be helpful.

CONVENTIONAL MEDICATION

If your vet prescribes a medication for your dog, don't leave the office without a clear understanding of what you're supposed to do with it. If there is something about the medication you don't understand, ask the vet. Here is the minimum of what you need to know about each medication your pet receives:

- What it is. You should know both the generic and trade name of the medication.
- What illness or disease it is being used to treat.
- When to give it and for how long.
- How it should be administered.
- What side effects it may have.
- How it interacts with any other medications your dog is receiving.

Dispensing Medication

Undoubtedly you will end up giving your dog medication from time to time. Doing it correctly assures that you are giving the right medication at the right time in the right dosage. The obvious first step is to follow your vet's instructions to the letter—the directions on the package may also help.

When purchasing medication, you should know that, as with human medicines, some kinds are available in generic form. These are almost always cheaper and usually of the same quality as the name brand. Although both products must meet minimum standards, sometimes the name brand does provide better ingredients. Ask your veterinarian about each specific drug.

You should not order medications and immunizations through the mail and administer them to the dog yourself, even if you know how to give injections. You may save some money, but in the long run you'll be doing your dog a disservice. This is because when you take the dog to the vet, you are doing more than getting him a shot and going home; this is a chance to speak with your vet about your concerns and observations. It's also important for the veterinarian to see your dog when he's healthy as well as when he's sick. This way, your vet can get a look at your "normal" GSD!

Taking Your Dog's Temperature

Although you won't be taking your dog's temperature every day, it's a good skill to learn in case you suspect anything is wrong with him. The first time you try it, it's best to work with a healthy animal.

Purchase a rectal thermometer specifically designed for dogs. Unfortunately, you can't use one of the stick-it-in-the-ear probes for dogs. The L-shape of a dog's ear canal makes an ear probe inaccurate. You'll have to do it the old-fashioned way. Clean the thermometer with alcohol and shake it down until it reads about 96°F. (Keep a moist towelette nearby to clean it afterward.) Then, lubricate the thermometer with mineral oil or petroleum jelly. Lift your German Shepherd's tail gently and place the end of the thermometer into the rectum. Slide slightly upward until it's halfway inserted, and keep it there for about two minutes. You may need someone to help hold the dog. Next, remove the instrument, wipe it, and read it. Normal canine temperature should read between 100.5° and 102.5°F or 38.1° and 39.2°C. Variation of more than 1 degree may warrant a call to your vet, especially if other symptoms are also present.

Ear Medication

Ear medications come in many forms: liquids, ointments, and powders. Every package has specific directions for how to administer that particular medication, so follow them carefully.

Eye Medication

To administer eye medication, stand behind the dog and place one hand on the side of his head to hold the head still and open the eye. Then, apply the medication with the other hand. Apply the required amount directly into the eye.

Pills

The trick to giving your dog pills is to do it so fast that the dog will be unaware he's been given a pill. In most cases, you can hide the pill in a bit of cheese, but if for some reason you can't do this, place your hand in the dog's mouth to open it and insert the pill at the base of the tongue. Once the pill is inserted, close the mouth and hold for a few seconds. You can also blow in his nose. This will force him to swallow.

ALTERNATIVE AND COMPLEMENTARY MEDICINE

Contemporary pet owners (and their vets) are no longer limited to conventional treatments. New ideas in medicine are pouring in from all around the world. Some of the "new ideas," by the way, are thousands of years old, and many are quite effective. However, you should seek the advice of your veterinarian before attempting an alternative therapy.

Acupuncture

Acupuncture has been used to treat animals for over 3,000 years! (One of the first acupuncture patients was supposedly an elephant who was healed of bloat by acupuncture.) Acupuncture is based on the idea that a flow of energy, or Qi (pronounced chee), empowers all living creatures. It flows through channels called meridians, which when stimulated at specific points (acupuncture points) help heal the body and promote wellness. It also works by restoring balance and enhancing the body's ability to heal itself.

As a complementary treatment, you can use acupuncture along with conventional treatments and medications. Your dog will probably enjoy the treatments—I have seen dogs actually fall asleep before the last needle was inserted.

Chiropractic Care

Chiropractic care is a mechanical, drug-free adjunct to (not replacement for) veterinary care. It is designed to decrease pain and improve movement and range of motion. It is typically used when trauma that has caused disruption to the normal workings of joints and muscles has occurred, and is also sometimes used in cases of arthritis, disk disease, Wobbler's syndrome, nerve problems, and hip dysplasia. Typically, chiropractors treat nerves pinched by a misaligned joint (a condition called a subluxation) or tight muscle. The chiropractor's job is to gently adjust the misaligned area. Animal chiropractors use much less force than is common with human patients. Usually a patient will need several visits, weeks or even months apart. When done correctly, chiropractic therapy can restore proper movement.

Chiropractic care can help get you and your dog back "in the swim."

Herbal Medicine

Many people favor traditional methods of healing these days, and one of the most popular methods of treating disease is through the use of herbal medications. In fact, worldwide, over 4 billion people use herbs as a regular part of medical care. And while herbs can indeed heal, they should not be used except in consultation with your holistic veterinarian or a qualified animal herbalist.

Herbs are not always effective, and they are not always safe. (The same is true for modern drugs, of course.) The fact that herbs are "natural" says nothing about their safety. Snake venom is natural, too. The U.S. Food and Drug Administration classifies herbs (and vitamins and minerals) as dietary supplements—not as drugs. Therefore, herbs are not subject to the rigorous safety tests that drugs must pass before being approved. Nor do herbal manufacturing companies need to follow the same quality-control standards as drug companies. Herbs can come in many forms, and depending upon which part of the plant is used and whether it is fresh or dry, whole or extracted, tincture or tea, the strength of the medication can vary. However, progress is being made. Good herbal products carry the USP (United States Pharmacopoeia) or NF (Natural Formulary) approval, which ensures that the product has been subjected to certain protocols for extracting or drying herbs. The best products also carry the stamp of approval from Consumer Lab (CL). These products have a guarantee of identity, purity, consistency, and potency.

If you are unsure how to properly administer medication to your GSD, ask your vet for a demonstration.

Don't begin experimenting with herbal medications without guidance, especially if your dog is already undergoing medical treatment. Many herbs can act adversely with drugs. Don't guess. If you do decide to use herbal supplements or herbal treatment, stick with just one or two until you can understand their effects.

Herbs are the source of most modern medications, so it would be surprising if they didn't have any beneficial effects. They are most effective for chronic problems, but don't expect them to work miracles.

Homeopathy

Homeopathy is a holistic system of medicine invented by Samuel Hahnemann, a German physician and chemist, about 200 years ago. Homeopathists believe that conventional medicine is too focused on signs and symptoms of disease rather than on the patient, who, they believe, often suffers due to a physical or emotional imbalance or instability.

Homeopathy is based on the old idea of "like cures like," and in fact the name homeopathy is derived from the Greek word "homios," which means "similar." Homeopathic medicines are natural substances (derived from plants or occasionally insects) prepared by a process of serial dilution (with water and alcohol) and succession, or repeated shaking. Homeopathists believe the shaking of the substance helps to conserve its energy and potency. The final product, which may contain extracts from more than one plant in pill or liquid form, has been diluted from ten times to millions of times.

In homeopathy, the more diluted the remedy, or medicine, the more potent it is believed to be. It seems counterintuitive that this should be so, but homeopathists swear by the results. Homeopathy does have the advantage of being inexpensive and free of side effects. It is most often used to help treat kidney and liver disease, arthritis, and hormonal imbalances.

T-Touch

One special kind of massage is Tellington TTouch, a kind of gentle body work designed to help an animal regain focus and balance.

Massage Therapy

Massage therapy is as good for dogs as it is for human beings. It provides a sense of calm well-being, increases movement and flexibility, improves circulation, and even helps reduce pain and stress. Studies suggest that massage therapy results in quicker post-surgical recovery, and it may help remove toxins from the system as well. However, massage is not advisable for animals with fever, shock, infection, lumps, rashes, or open wounds. Like most complementary therapies, massage is not intended as a substitute for veterinary care, but as an adjunct to it.

Massage involves applying gentle pressure (from 5 grams to 5 pounds) to specific parts of the body. The amount of pressure depends on the dog's size and particular needs.

You can learn some simple massage techniques yourself, or for more advanced care, you may wish to take your dog to a certified practitioner who is trained in canine anatomy and movement.

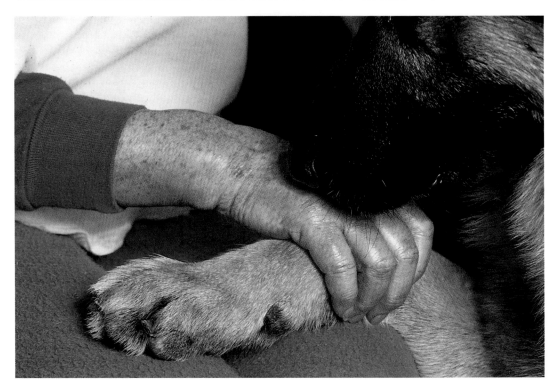

Passive touch is a massage therapy technique that warms the tissue and pacifies the dog.

Knowledge of anatomy is very important, because every muscle in the body affects every other muscle. Various different massage techniques can be used, including the following.

Effleurage

Effleurage encourages better circulation. With this technique, the therapist uses rotary, one-hand and hand-over-hand movement from head to tail over the entire body, down the outside, and up the inside of the limbs. It's frequently used at the beginning or close of a session.

Passive Touch

Passive touch requires neither pressure nor hand movement. The hand is simply held in place for 30 to 90 seconds to warm the tissue and pacify the dog. It may be used at any point during the massage.

Kneading

Kneading can be applied either superficially or deeply. Superficial kneading involves skin rolling and manipulation to stimulate the skin and hair coat. It also increases blood circulation. Deep kneading is applied directly to the muscle and manipulates the muscle fiber; this helps transport blood and nutrients to the muscle and removes toxins. It also decreases or eliminates muscle spasms.

Tapotement

Tapotement is a treatment suitable for a cheerful dog with no fear or history of abuse. It involves various kinds of quick tapping or light striking motions on various parts of the body. Cupping, for instance, is used on the chest to loosen mucus in the lungs. Hacking (a light chopping motion) loosens large muscle areas, while tapping is used on large muscle areas, but not on the spine. Brushing is used on all muscle groups.

Stroking

Stroking is a gentle, slow petting used to calm and quiet the animal. This is a closing technique.

The golden years can be the best you spend with your friend; make them last by giving your old dog what he needs for his aging body and mind.

Passive Joint Movement

Passive joint movement and stretching is a range of motion physical therapy for the moveable joints. Positioning is important. If done incorrectly, this technique can cause trauma to the joints and tissues and is best used under professional guidance.

THE SENIOR GERMAN SHEPHERD DOG

Over 14 percent of pet dogs are over the age of 11! If you want your German Shepherd to be among this crowd, you should start pampering him now.

Nutrition

As dogs age, their digestive systems often don't function as well as before. For one thing, their production of digestive juices declines. Older dogs also may require as much as 50 percent more protein than young adults. This is

Your senior GSD deserves the extra attention he should be getting in his old age. A soft bed, extra sleep, proper nutrition, and your full attention will all help him age gracefully.

because older dogs are less able to metabolize protein, so more needs to be added to the diet.

When your German Shepherd reaches the age of six, switch him to an appropriate senior diet, which should include the necessary higher levels of protein for older dogs. Most senior diets contain less fat and calories than adult food, not because the dog's essential metabolism has changed, but because most older dogs lead a more sedentary life and simply burn up fewer calories. Some of these diets also have lower cholesterol and add essential fatty acids.

Older dogs can frequently benefit from vitamin supplements, especially the antioxidants A, C, and E, as well as glucosamine and chondroitin sulfate for arthritic dogs. Ask your veterinarian for advice.

Training

Although it may indeed be too late to teach an old dog new tricks, it's not too late to keep your oldster up and about with plenty of age-appropriate exercise. Primarily, this means taking your dog for walks with you. Consider the walks not only good for your dog's physical health but a chance to solidify the bond between you, to dream of other days, and simply to enjoy each other's company.

In addition, reviewing basic obedience commands is a good way to give him attention and remind him that he is still a part of the "pack" with an important role to play.

Golden Age Comfort

If you treat your elderly GSD like the king he is, you'll not only help him live longer, you'll help him live happier as well.

A raised, soft, comfortable bed positioned away from drafts will help your German Shepherd sleep better and restore his energy more efficiently. If you have the time, give him a nice gentle massage when he wakes up; this will help get his circulation going and relieve cramps. Gentle stretching exercises will also help, especially just before a walk.

Keep exercising your dog at a moderate level, being careful to avoid rough, hard surfaces.

Death and Renewal

All beings must pass away, and unfortunately, the beautiful German Shepherd Dog passes all too soon. The experience of losing a beloved pet is undoubtedly one of life's more painful moments, but it can be eased by knowing how well you cared for your dog, how much you loved each other, and that the memories will remain.

In most cases nowadays, you will know in advance that your dog's time to die is near, and it will be up to you to take him to the vet and be with him when that time actually comes. Some owners do not feel up to being in the room during euthanasia, and if you are one of these, rest assured that your dog's old friend, the vet, will make his passing easy and painless. On the other hand, you may wish to brave it out and hold your dog until the last. Whatever decision you make, it will be the right one for you.

The deep bond you develop over a lifetime with your dog is something that will stay with you forever.

You can commemorate your dog's passing in many ways. You might want to make a donation to a German Shepherd Dog rescue in your dog's name. You might wish to hold a service, take some time off, write a poem, or construct a memory garden. Your grieving period is both a tribute to your dog and a chance for you to heal.

Some people decide to get a new puppy or adopt an older dog very soon after the passing of their pet. Others prefer to wait months or even years. Some vow earnestly they will never get another dog, because it was too painful to lose the first. For most dog lovers, though, life without a dog is not to be contemplated. Just remember that your new dog will not be a clone of your old one. Every dog is an individual, a unique creation that has never been before and will never be again. Love and enjoy your new German Shepherd Dog for the renewed spirit he brings to you. He is a priceless gift.

The German Shepherd Dog

ORGANIZATIONS

American Kennel Club (AKC)
5580 Centerview Drive
Raleigh, NC 27606
Telephone: (919) 233-9767
Fax: (919) 233-3627
E-mail: info@akc.org
www.akc.org

Association of Pet Dog Trainers (APDT)
150 Executive Center Drive
Box 35
Greenville, SC 29615
Telephone: (800) PET-DOGS
Fax: (864) 331-0767
www.apdt.com

Canadian Kennel Club (CKC)
89 Skyway Avenue, Suite 100
Etobicoke, Ontario M9W 6R4
Telephone: (416) 675-5511
Fax: (416) 675-6506
E-mail: information@ckc.ca
www.ckc.ca

Delta Society
875 124th Ave NE, suite 101
Bellevue, WA 98005
Telephone: (425) 226-7357
Fax: (425) 235-1076
E-mail: info@deltasociety.org
www.deltasociety.org

German Shepherd Dog Club of America (GSDCA)
Secretary: Sharon Allbright
E-mail: sharlen@foothill.net
www.gsdca.org

German Shepherd Dog Club of America-Working Dog Association
GSDCA-WDA Central Office
1699 N. Jungle Den Rd. #45
Astor, FL 32102
Telephone: (386) 749-4574
Fax: (386) 749-1013
E-mail: joy@usa2net.net
www.gsdca-wda.org

International Agility Link (IAL)
Global Administrator:
Steve Drinkwater
E-mail: yunde@powerup.au
www.agilityclick.com/~ial

North American Flyball Association (NAFA)
1400 West Devon Avenue #512
Chicago, IL 60660
Telephone: (800) 318-6312
Fax: (800) 318-6318
www.flyball.org

North American Ski Joring Association
Secretary: Kitty LeDonne
E-mail: kitty@nasja.com
www.nasja.com

American White Shepherd Association
Secretary: Pam Hovind
E-mail: info@awsaclub.com
www.awsaclub.com

British Association for German Shepherd Dogs
Membership Secretary: Mrs. D. Little
E-mail: bagsd@freeuk.com
www.bagsd.com

The Kennel Club (UK)
1 Clarges Street
London
W1J 8AB
Telephone: 0870 606 6750
Fax: 0207 518 1058
www.the-kennel-club.org.uk

United Kennel Club (UKC)
100 E. Kilgore Road
Kalamazoo, MI 49002-5584
Telephone: (269) 343-9020
Fax: (269) 343-7037
E-mail: pbickell@ukcdogs.com
www.ukcdogs.com

United Schutzhund Clubs of America
3810 Paule Ave.
St. Louis, MO 63125
Telephone: (314) 638-9686
Fax: (314) 638-0609
E-mail: usaoffice@germanshepherddog.com
www.germanshepherddog.com

Verein Für Deutsche Schäferhunde (SV) E.V.
Häuptgeschaftsstelle
Steinerne Furt 71,
86167 Augsburg, Germany
Telephone: 0821 740020
Fax: 0821 74002 903
E-Mail: info@schaeferhunde.de
www.schaeferhund.de/sv_start_english.htm

White German Shepherd Dog Club International, Inc.
Recording Secretary: Nancy H. Swanner
E-mail: RecordingSecretary@whitegermanshepherd.org
www.whitegermanshepherd.org

White German Shepherd Dog Club of America (WGSDCA)
Secretary: Elaine Hurrle
E-mail: boonerbutt@yahoo.com
www.wgsdca.org

World Canine Freestyle Organization
P.O. Box 350122
Brooklyn, NY 11235-2525
Telephone: (718) 332-8336
Fax: (718) 646-2686
E-mail: wcfodogs@aol.com
www.worldcaninefreestyle.org

INTERNET RESOURCES

Herding on the Web
(www.herdingontheweb.com)
This site covers every topic related to training a dog to herd. The extensive list of media resources, international clubs, and herding techniques will help GSD owners learn to teach their companions this skill.

German Shepherd World (www.gsdworld.net)
This site is an international forum that allows GSD owners from every part of the globe to connect and discuss every topic relating to their beloved GSDs, including diet, nutrition, training, health issues, conformation, and more.

PUBLICATIONS:
Books

Anderson, Teoti. *The Super Simple Guide to Housetraining.* Neptune City: T.F.H. Publications, Inc. 2004

Goldstein, Dr. Robert and Susan. *The Goldsteins' Wellness and Longevity Program for Dogs and Cats.* Neptune City: T.F.H. Publications, Inc. 2005

Yin, Dr. Sophia. *How to Behave So Your Dog Behaves.* Neptune City: T.F.H. Publications, Inc. 2004

Magazines

AKC Family Dog
American Kennel Club
260 Madison Avenue
New York, NY 10016
Telephone: (800) 490-5675
E-mail: familydog@akc.org
www.akc.org/pubs/familydog

AKC Gazette
American Kennel Club
260 Madison Avenue
New York, NY 10016
Telephone: (800) 533-7323
E-mail: gazette@akc.org
www.akc.org/pubs/gazette

Dog & Kennel
Pet Publishing, Inc.
7-L Dundas Circle
Greensboro, NC 27407
Telephone: (336) 292-4272
Fax: (336) 292-4272
E-mail: info@petpublishing.com
www.dogandkennel.com

Dog Fancy
Subscription Department
P.O. Box 53264
Boulder, CO 80322-3264
Telephone: (800) 365-4421
E-mail: barkback@dogfancy.com
www.dogfancy.com

Dogs Monthly
Ascot House
High Street, Ascot,
Berkshire SL5 7JG
United Kingdom
Telephone: 0870 730 8433
Fax: 0870 730 8431
E-mail: admin@rtc-associates.freeserve.co.uk
www.corsini.co.uk/dogsmonthly

The German Shepherd Quarterly
4401 Zephyr St.
Wheat Ridge, CO 80033
Telephone: (303) 420-2222
Fax: (720) 207-0382

The German Shepherd Review
1902C N. Abrego
Green Valley, AZ 85614
Telephone: (520) 625-9528
Fax: (520) 625-4789
E-mail: gsreview@cox.net
www.gsdca.org/Noframes/review.html

Working Dogs Cyberzine
Fax: (719) 570-7097
E-mail:
www.workingdogs.com/contactus.htm
www.workingdogs.com

ANIMAL WELFARE GROUPS AND RESCUE ORGANIZATIONS

American German Shepherd Rescue Association, Inc.
6565 Buena O'Brien
Magalia, CA 95954
E-mail: lindakury@saber.net
Telephone: (630) 529-7396
www.agsra.com

American Humane Association (AHA)
63 Inverness Drive East
Englewood, CO 80112
Telephone: (303) 792-9900
Fax: 792-5333
www.americanhumane.org

American Society for the Prevention of Cruelty to Animals (ASPCA)
424 E. 92nd Street
New York, NY 10128-6804
Telephone: (212) 876-7700
www.aspca.org

Royal Society for the Prevention of Cruelty to Animals (RSPCA)
Telephone: 0870 3335 999
Fax: 0870 7530 284
www.rspca.org.uk

The Humane Society of the United States (HSUS)
2100 L Street, NW
Washington DC 20037
Telephone: (202) 452-1100
www.hsus.org

UK National German Shepherd Dog Help Line
www.gsdhelpline.com
World Animal Net (USA)
19 Chestnut Square
Boston, MA 02130
Telephone: (617) 524-3670
E-mail: info@worldanimal.net
www.worldanimal.net

World Animal Net (UK)
24 Barleyfields
Didcot, Oxon OX11 OBJ
Telephone: + 44 1235 210 775
E-mail: info@worldanimal.net
www.worldanimal.net

VETERINARY RESOURCES

American Academy of Veterinary Acupuncture (AAVA)
66 Morris Avenue, Suite 2A
Springfield, NJ 07081
Telephone: (973) 379-1100
E-mail: office@aava.org
www.aava.org

American Animal Hospital Association (AAHA)
P.O. Box 150899
Denver, CO 80215-0899
Telephone: (303) 986-2800
Fax: (303) 986-1700
E-mail: info@aahanet.org
www.aahanet.org

American College of Veterinary Ophthalmologists (ACVO)
P.O. Box 1311
Mediridan, Idaho 83680
Telephone: (208) 466-7624
E-mail: office@acvo.org
www.acvo.com

American Veterinary Chiropractic Association (AVCA)
442154 E 140 Rd.
Bluejacket, OK 74333
Telephone: (918) 784-2231
E-mail: amvetchiro@aol.com
www.animalchiropractic.org

American Veterinary Medical Association (AVMA)
1931 North Meacham Road
Schaumburg, IL 60173
Telephone: (847) 925-8070
Fax: (847) 925-1329
E-mail: avmainfo@avma.org
www.avma.org

British Veterinary Association (BVA)
7 Mansfield Street
London
W1G 9NQ
Telephone: 020 7636 6541
Fax: 020 7436 2970
E-mail: bvahq@bva.co.uk
www.bva.co.uk

Note: Boldface numbers indicate illustrations; an italic *t* indicates a table.

A

accidents in housetraining, 101
acupuncture, 193
Addison's disease, 85, 168–169
adenovirus-2 in, 147
adult dog adoption, 41–42
adverse reactions to vaccines, 151
aggression, 112–115
agility competition, 132, 133–134, **134**
agouti coloration, 31
allergies, 166
    vaccination and, 151
Alsatian Wolf Dog, 11
alternative (holistic) and comple-
    mentary medicine, 175, 192–197
American Herding Breeds
    Association (AHBA), 138
American Kennel Club (AKC), 13,
    22
    Canine Good Citizen (CGC)
        program, 127
    conformation shows sanctioned
        by, 128
American Veterinary Medical
    Association (AVMA), 141
anal sac impaction, 180
anaphylaxis, 151
anti-chew spray, 60
aortic stenosis, 165
Apollo von Hunenstein, 14
appearance, 49
arthritis, 85, 177–178
artificial flavors and preservatives
    in, 80
ASPCA, 141
Association of American Feed
    Control Officials (AAFCO), 78
Axel von der Deininghauserheide,
    11

B

babesiosis, 153
baby gates, 59–60
bad breath (halitosis), 166
barking, 115–116
bathing, 89–90
beds and bedding, 56
Begleithund (BH) test, 12
Belgium Sheepdog, 13
Bernd von Kallengarten, 15
bleeding, 181–182
bloat (gastric torsion and stomach
    distension) in, 182–183, 185
boarding your German Shepherd
    Dog, 65–67
body language, staring, 112
body, 26–27
bonding with your German
    Shepherd Dog, 37–38
bones and joints
    arthritis in, 177–178

degenerative myelopathy in, 179
elbow dysplasia in, 14, 15, 180
hip dysplasia in, 14, 15, 51,
    179–180
passive joint movement therapy
    in, 197
bones in diet, 82–84
bordetellosis (kennel cough), 147,
    150
bowls for food and water, 55
breathing difficulties, 187–188
breed registries, 12
breed standards, 6–7, 21–22
    variations by country of origin
        in, 19–21
breeders, 42–45
British Association for German
    Shepherd Dogs (BAGSD), 11–12
British Schutzhund Association
    (BSA), 12, 135–136
brushes and brushing, 87–88, **88**
brushing your dog's teeth, 92–93
by-products, in foods, 81

C

Canada and the German Shepherd
    Dog, 13
cancer, 164
canine cognitive dysfunction
    (CCD), 175
Canine Companions for
    Independence, 139
Canine Good Citizen (CGC) pro-
    gram, 127
canned dog food, 82
car chasing, 120–121
car travel, seat belts and restraints
    for, 60
carbohydrates in diet, 72–73
cardiovascular (heart) disease,
    164–165
cataracts, 14, 171–172
chewing, 58–59, 60, 117–118
Cheyletiella yasguri (walking dan-
    druff), 156
children and the German Shepherd
    Dog, **62**, 63
chiropractic care, 193
chocolate, 84
choke collars, 56–57
cleaning up accidents, 101
clubs and associations, 11–12
coat and skin, 28–30. *See also*
    grooming
    allergies and, 162–164
    hot spots in, 163
    mites and mange in, 155–157
    pyoderma in, 163–164
    ringworm in, 159–160
    shedding and, 30, 88
collars, 56–57, 102
color, 30–31
    nose, 25
    white, 14, 24, 30–31, 33–36, **33**,
        35
come command, 103–104, **103**
commercial dog foods, 79–81

conformation showing, 8, 128–130
    American Kennel Club (AKC)
        and, 128
    German rules for, 129–130
    handlers for, 128–129
    match-type, 130
    white German Shepherd Dog
        and, 35
ConsumerLab (CL) seal of
    approval, 75
contracts, 51–52
corncobs, 85
coronavirus, 147, 148*t*, 150
CPR for your dog, 187–188
crates, 54–55
cruciate ligament injuries, 85
Cushing's disease, 85, 119, 169

D

dancing with dogs, 138–139
dandruff, walking, 156
degenerative myelopathy, 179
Demodex mange, 155–156
dental care, 92–93, **93**, 166
    bad breath (halitosis) and, 166
diabetes, 85, 169–171
diarrhea, 173
digging, 116
disqualifications from show,
    according to country, 32
distemper, 147
Dog Act of 1906 (UK), 55
dog foods, 79–81
doggie doors, 55
Doris Day Animal League, 141
down command, 107, **108**
drop it command, 105–106
dry eye (keratoconjunctivitis sicca),
    172
dry food or kibble, 81

E

ears and ear care, 24–25, 91–92, 157,
    166–168, 192
ear mites, 157
early development of the breed,
    5–7
effleurage (massage), 196
ehrlichiosis, 153, 157
elbow dysplasia, 14, 15, 180
emergencies, 180
end-of-life issues, 198–199
England and the German Shepherd
    Dog, 11–12
epilepsy, 14, 175–176, 189
essential fatty acids (EFAs), 71
exercise pens, 60
exercise requirements, 37, 65, 198
eyes and eye care, 24, 92, 171–173,
    192
    cataracts in, 171–172
    dry eye (keratoconjunctivitis
        sicca) in, 172
    pannus (Uberreiter's disease) in,
        172–173

F

fats in diet, 71–72
fears and phobias, 118–119
federal agency dogs, 140
Federal Property and Administrative Services Act of 1979, 140–141
Federation Cynologique Internationale (FCI), 21, 22
feeding, 65, 69–85
  allergies and, 162–164, 166
  artificial flavors and preservatives in, 80
  bloat (gastric torsion and stomach distension) and, 182–183, 185
  bones in, 82–84
  bowls for, 55
  by-products in, 81
  canned foods in, 82
  carbohydrates in, 72–73
  commercial dog foods in, 79–81
  diarrhea and, 173
  dry food or kibble in, 81
  fats and EFAs in, 71–72
  fiber in, 73
  generic vs. named brands in, 81
  homemade foods in, 82–83
  immune function and, 72
  labeled contents of dog food in, 78–79
  meat meal in, 80
  methods for, free, timed, vs. food-restricted, 76–77
  minerals and vitamins in, 73–76
  obesity and, 85
  proteins in, 70–71
  raw diets (BARF diet) in, 82–83
  recommended daily allowance (RDA) and, 70
  semi-moist foods in, 82
  senior dogs, 197–198
  storage containers for, 55, 84
  supplements and, 75
  toxic foods and materials in, 61–64, 84–85
  treats and, 83
  vomiting and, 174
  water requirements and, 70
femoral head and neck ostectomy (FHO), 179
fiber in diet, 73
first-aid kit, 184
fleas, 151, 152–163, 162
Flora Berkemeyer, 14
flyball competition, 132, 136–137
Food and Drug Administration (FDA) and dog foods, 78
food-restricted feedings, 77
forequarters, 27–28
formal training, 109–111
free feeding, 76–77
Frisbee, 143
frostbite, 186–187

G

gait, 31–32
games for your German Shepherd Dog, 142–143
gastric torsion and stomach distension (bloat), 182–183, 185
gastroenteritis, 173–174
generally accepted as safe (in foods), 78
generic vs. named brands, dog foods, 81
German language commands, 105
German Shepherd Dog Club of Canada, 13
German Shepherd Dog Club of America (GSDCA), 14, 21
German Shepherd Dog League of Great Britain (GSDL), 12, 136
Germany and the German Shepherd Dog, 5–6, 20–21, 129–130
giardia, 160
give it/drop it command, 105–106
goals of training, 101
Good Manufacturing Practices Certificate (GMP), 75
grapes and raisins, 84
Grief, 33
grooming, 37, 87–93
  bathing in, 89–90
  brushes and brushing in, 87–88, 88
  dental care in, 92–93, 93
  ear care in, 91–92
  eye care in, 92
  nail care in, 90–91, 90
  shedding and, 88
  supplies for, 59, 87
  trimming in, 88
guide dogs, 139–140
Guiding Eyes for the Blind, 139

H

haemobartonellosis, 153
halters, 56–57
handler selection, for showing, 128–129
harnesses, 57
head halters, 56
head, 24–25
health issues, 15, 44–45, 65, 145–199
  acupuncture in, 193
  adenovirus-2 in, 147
  adverse reactions to vaccines and, 151
  allergies in, 162–164
  alternative (holistic) and complementary medicine in, 175, 192–197
  anal sac impaction in, 180
  anaphylaxis in, 151
  aortic stenosis in, 165
  arthritis in, 85, 177–178
  bleeding in, 181–182
  bloat (gastric torsion and stomach distension) in, 182–183, 185
  bordetellosis (kennel cough) in, 147, 150
  breathing difficulty in, 187–188
  cancer in, 164
  canine cognitive dysfunction (CCD) in, 175
  cardiovascular (heart) disease in, 164–165
  cataracts, 14, 171–172
  chiropractic care in, 193
  coronavirus in, 147, 148t, 150
  CPR in, 187–188
  cruciate ligament injuries and, 85
  Cushing's disease as, 119
  degenerative myelopathy in, 179
  dental care and, 92–93, 93, 166
  diabetes and, 85, 169–171
  diarrhea in, 173
  distemper in, 147
  dry eye (keratoconjunctivitis sicca) in, 172
  ear care in, 91–92, 166–168, 192
  ear mites and, 157
  ehrlichiosis in, 157
  elbow dysplasia, 14, 15, 180
  emergencies, 180
  end-of-life issues in, 198–199
  epilepsy in, 14, 175–176, 189
  eye care in, 92, 171–173, 192
  first-aid kit for, 184
  fleas in, 151, 152–153
  gastroenteritis in, 173–174
  giardia in, 160
  heartworm in, 152, 161
  heat exhaustion/heatstroke in, 185–186
  hepatitis in, 147, 149
  herbal medicine in, 193–194
  hip dysplasia, 14, 15, 51, 179–180
  homeopathy in, 195
  hookworm in, 151, 159
  hot spots in, 163
  hyperadrenocorticism (Cushing's disease) in, 85, 169
  hypoadrenocorticism (Addison's disease) in, 85, 168–169
  hypothermia/frostbite in, 186–187
  hypothyroidism in, 85, 171
  immune function, diet and, 72
  insect bites and stings in, 181
  kidney (renal) disease in, 174–175
  leptospirosis in, 147, 148t, 149–150
  Lyme disease in, 147, 148t, 150–151, 153
  massage therapy in, 195–197
  medical records and, 51
  medication administration/dispensing in, 191–192
  minerals and vitamins in, 73–76
  mites and mange in, 151, 155–157
  obesity and, 85
  obsessive-compulsive disorder (OCD) as, 119–120
  osteochondrosis dissecans and, 85

pannus (Uberreiter's disease) in, 172–173
parainfluenza in, 147
parasites in, 151–161
parvovirus in, 147, 148t, 148–149
poisoning in, 188
pyoderma in, 163–164
rabies and, 146, 148t
ringworm in, 159–160
roundworm in, 151, 158
seizures in, 14, 175–176, 189–190. *See also* epilepsy
senior dogs and, 197–199
separation anxiety as, 121–124
spaying and neutering in, 51, 147
stroke in, 190
supplements and, 75
tapeworm in, 151, 158
temperature-taking in, 192
ticks in, 151, 153–155
vaccinations and, 145–151, 148t
veterinarian selection and vet visits for, 145
vital signs in, normal numbers for, 189
vomiting in, 174
von Willebrand's disease, 14
whipworm in, 151, 159
white color and, 34
worms and worming in, 151, 158–161
heart disease, 164–165
Heart von Ehrengrund, 14
heartworm, 152, 161
heat exhaustion/heatstroke in, 185–186
heel command, 108–109
Hein vom Richterbach, 11
Hektor Kinksrhein, 5
hepatitis, 147, 149
hepatozoonosis, 153
herbal medicine, 193–194
herding competition, 137–138, **137**
hindquarters, 28
hip dysplasia, 14, 15, 51, 179–180
history of the German Shepherd Dog, 5
holistic medicine. *See* alternative (holistic) and complementary medicine
homemade foods, 82–83
homeopathy, 195
hookworm, 151, 159
Horhand von Grafrath, 5, 33
hot spots, 163
house sitters, 66
housetraining, 97–101
housing requirements, 37
Humane Society of the United States, 141
hyperadrenocorticism (Cushing's disease), 85, 169
hypoadrenocorticism (Addison's disease), 85, 168–169
hypothermia/frostbite, 186–187

hypothyroidism, 85, 171

I
identification tags, 56
immune function and diet, 72
insect bites and stings, 181

J
jogging with your German Shepherd Dog, 142–143

K
Kennel Club, 11–12, 132
kennel cough. *See* bordetella
kennels, boarding, 66–67
keratoconjunctivitis sicca, 172
kibble, 81
kidney (renal) disease, 174–175
Klodo von Boxberg, 8–9, 15
kneading (massage), 196–197

L
labeled contents of dog food, 78–79
leashes and leads, 57–58
leptospirosis, 147, 148t, 149–150
limited registration, 51
Long Worth bloodlines, 33
lost dogs, 67
Luchs (Lux), 14
Lyme disease, 147, 148t, 150–151, 153

M
male vs. female, 42
Maraldene Kennels, 9
massage therapy, 195–197
match-type shows, 130
meat meals, in food, 80
medication administration/dispensing in, 191–192
Meyer, Arthur, 5
microchipping, 56
military dogs, 140
minerals and vitamins, 73–76
Mira of Dalmore, 13
mites and mange, 151, 155–157
mixed messages and commands, 106
movies, tv, and the German Shepherd Dog, 10
multiple dogs, 54
musical freestyle competition, 138–139
muzzle, 25

N
nail care, 90–91, **90**
naming your German Shepherd Dog, 5
National Research Council (NRC), 70
Nazi regime and the German Shepherd Dog, 10–11
neck, 26–27
no command, 104–105
noise phobias, 118–119
nose, 24, 25

Nylabone, 55, 56, 84, 93

O
obedience competition, 131–133
obesity, 85
obsessive-compulsive disorder (OCD), 119–120
off command, 105
onions, 84–85
Orthopedic Foundation for Animals (OFA), 179
osteochondrosis dissecans, 85

P
pannus (Uberreiter's disease), 172–173
paperwork involved in puppy purchase, 51–52
parainfluenza, 147
parasites, 151–161. *See also* fleas; worms and worming
parvovirus, 147, 148t, 148–149
passive joint movement therapy, 197
passive touch therapy, 196
Peabody Museum, Yale, 14
PennHIP program, 179
pet sitters, Pet Sitters International, 67
pet store puppies, 48–49
pet vs. show quality dogs, 44
pets and the German Shepherd Dog, 38
Pfeffer von Bern (Ch.), 15
phobias, 118–119
Phylax Society, 7
pilling your dog, 191–192
please leave command, 109
Poison Control Hotline Number, 188
poisoning, 188
police dogs, 8, 140
pooper-scoopers, 55
positive reinforcement in training, 95–96
preservatives in food, 80
problem behaviors, 111–125
    aggression as, 112–115
    barking as, 115–116
    car chasing as, 120–121
    chewing as, 117–118
    "cures" for, 112
    digging as, 116
    drug therapies for, 121–122
    noise phobias as, 118–119
    obsessive-compulsive disorder (OCD) as, 119–120
    running away as, 120–121
    separation anxiety as, 121–124
    shyness as, 124–125
professional trainers, 109–111
protection dogs, 7, 38. *See also* Schutzhund
proteins in diet, 70–71
puppies
    adult adoption vs., 41–42

breeder screening for, 42–45
chewing and, 58–59
choosing, 41–42, 49–51
health issues and, 44–45
housetraining and, 97–101
male vs. female, 42
paperwork involved in purchase
    of, 51–52
pet stores as source for, 48–49
pet vs. show quality, 44
puppy-proofing your home for,
    61–64
rescues and shelters as sources
    of, 45–47
routines for, 52–53
socialization and, 96–97
spaying and neutering of, 51, 147
supplies for, 54–56
temperament of, 49–51
training for, 53–54
vaccinations and, 145–146, 148t
puppy-proofing your home, 61–64
pyoderma, 163–164

Q
Queen of Switzerland, 13

R
rabies, 146, 148t
rally obedience competition, 133
raw diets (BARF diet), 82–83
recommended daily allowance
    (RDA), 70
registering your German Shepherd
    Dog, 12, 51
renal (kidney) disease, 174–175
rescue organizations, 45–47
Riego, Frank, 11
Rin Tin Tin, 9, 10, 33
ringworm, 159–160
Rocky Mountain Spotted Fever, 153
Rolf vom Osnabruker–Land, 11
roundworm, 151, 158
routines for your German Shepherd
    Dog, 52–53, 65
running away, 120–121

S
sarcoptic mange in, 156
scabies, 156
Schutzhund (protection dog) work,
    7, 20, 134–136, 135
search-and-rescue dogs, 141–142,
    141
seat belts, restraints, 60
seizures, 14, 189–190
self-sufficiency of the German
    Shepherd Dog, 38
semi-moist foods, 82
senior dogs
    end-of-life issues in, 198–199
    exercise requirements of, 198
    feeding, 197–198
    health issues, health care in,
        197–199
    training for, 111, 198

separation anxiety, 121–124
service dogs, 39, 39, 139–142
shedding, 30, 88
shelters, 45–47
show vs. pet/working dogs, 15–17,
    44
shyness, 124–125
sit command, 106–107
size, proportion, substance, 23–24
sleep requirements, 65
snow nose, 24
socialization, 96–97
spaying and neutering, 51, 147
sporting events, Kennel Club, 132
staring at your dog, 112
stay command, 106–107, 107
stings, insects/spiders, 181
Stonihurst Edmund, Eric, Eadred,
    Elf, 34
storage containers for food, 55, 84
stroke, 190
stroking (massage), 197
Strongheart, 9, 10, 33
supplements, 75
supplies, 54–56
SV, 12

T
tail, 27
tapeworm, 151, 158
tapotement (massage), 197
teeth and jaw, 25–26. See also dental
    care
temperament, 15, 23, 36, 49–51,
    124–125, 135–136
temperature-taking, 192
tick paralysis, 153
ticks, 151, 153–155
time feedings, 77
topline, 26–27
total hip replacement (THR), 179
toxic foods, materials, 61–64, 84–85,
    188
toys, 58–59
tracking competition, 133
Tracy, Ann, 34
training, 37, 65, 95–125
    collars for, 102
    come command in, 103–104, 103
    down command in, 107, 108
    German language commands in,
        105
    give it/drop it command in,
        105–106
    goal setting in, 101
    heel command in, 108–109
    housetraining and, 97–101
    mixed messages and commands
        in, 106
    no command in, 104–105
    off command in, 105
    please leave command in, 109
    positive reinforcement in, 95–96
    problem behaviors and. See prob-
        lem behaviors

professional trainers for, 109–111
    puppies and, 53–54
    senior dogs and, 111, 198
    sit command in, 106–107
    socialization and, 96–97
    stay command in, 106–107, 107
    watch me command in, 103
traveling with your German
    Shepherd Dog, 65–66
treats, 83
trimming the coat, 88
triple pelvic osteotomy (TPO), 179
Troll von Richterbach, 15–16, 15
tug-of-war games, 143
types of German Shepherd Dog
    breeds, 19–21

U
Uberreiter's disease (pannus),
    172–173
United Kingdom and the German
    Shepherd Dog, 11–12, 20, 21
United States and the German
    Shepherd Dog, 5, 11, 13–15, 20,
    21

V
V. Oerigen Strongheart, 33
vaccinations, 145–151
Verein fur Deutsche Schaferhunde
    (SV), 6–11
veterinarian selection and vet visits,
    145
vital signs, normal numbers for, 189
vitamins and minerals, 73–76
Vogt, Adolph, 13
vomiting, 174
von Stephanitz, Max Emil
    Frederich, 5–7, 17, 20, 33
von Willebrand's disease, 14

W
walking dandruff, 156
walking with your German
    Shepherd Dog, 108–109, 142–143
watch me command, 103
water requirements, 70
whipworm, 151, 159
White and Long Coat Shepherd
    Society, 36
white German Shepherd Dog, 14,
    24, 30–31, 33–36, 33, 35
working German Shepherd Dog,
    7–8
working trials, 132
working vs. show dogs, 15–17
World Union for German Shepherd
    Dogs (WUSV), 12, 136
World Wars I and II and the
    German Shepherd Dog, 9–11
worms and worming, 151, 158–161

X
xylitol, 61

DEDICATION
For Wayne Stidham and Katie.
In memory of Rittmeister Max Emil Frederich von Stephanitz, with profound gratitude.

ACKOWLEDGEMENTS
Thanks so much to Heather Russell-Revesz for thinking of me for this book
and to Stephanie Fornino for her expert and compassionate editing…as always,
you guys are the very best.

ABOUT THE AUTHOR

Diane Morgan is an assistant professor of philosophy and religion at Wilson College,
Chambersburg, PA. She has authored numerous books on canine care and nutrition and
has also written many dog breed books, horse books, and books on Eastern philosophy
and religion. She is an avid gardener (and writes about that, too). Diane lives in
Williamsport, Maryland, with several dogs, two cats, some fish, and a couple of humans.

PHOTO CREDITS
Photo on page 6 courtesy of Lara Stern
Photos on pages 39 and 140 courtesy of Tara Darling
Photo on page 130 courtesy of Judith E. Strom
Photo on page 139 courtesy of Liz Palika
All other photos courtesy of Isabelle Francais and T.F.H. archives

Nylabone® Cares.

Millions of dogs of all ages, breeds, and sizes have enjoyed our world-famous chew bones—but we're not just bones! Nylabone®, the leader in responsible animal care for over 50 years®, devotes the same care and attention to our many other award-winning, high-quality innovative products. Your dog will love them — and so will you!

Toys   Treats   Chews   Crates   Grooming